Experience Godliness
God's Way

*Revealing the Biblical Pattern for
Spiritual Growth & Christ-like Attitudes*

―――― Sarah Goebel ――――

www.OnAssignmentPublishing.com

Experience Godliness God's Way

Copyright © 2010 by Sarah Ann Goebel

ISBN: 978-0-9842428-5-6

Printed in the United States of America

All rights reserved. No part of this publication may be reproduced or transmitted in any form or by any means without written permission of the publisher.

Author's emphasis added to cited verses is shown in parentheses.

Unless otherwise indicated, Bible quotations are taken from the HOLY BIBLE, NEW INTERNATIONAL VERSION® Copyright © 1973, 1978, 1984 International Bible Society. Used by permission of Zondervan. All rights reserved.

Scripture quotations marked (NASB) are taken from the NEW AMERICAN STANDARD BIBLE®, Copyright ©1960, 1962, 1963, 1968, 1971, 1972, 1973, 1975, 1977,1995 by Lockman Foundation. Used by permission.

Scripture quotations marked (AMP) are taken from the AMPLIFIED® BIBLE, Copyright © 1954, 1958, 1962, 1964, 1965, 1987 by The Lockman Foundation. Used by permission. (www.Lockman.org).

Scripture quotations marked (NKJV) are taken from the NEW KING JAMES VERSION. Copyright © 1982 by Thomas Nelson, Inc. Used by permission. All rights reserved.

Scripture Quotations marked (MSG) are taken from THE MESSAGE BIBLE Copyright © 1993, 1994, 1995, 1996, 2000, 2001, 2002 by Eugene H. Peterson.

Scripture Quotations marked (NLT) are taken from the NEW LIVING TRANSLATION copyright © 1996, 2004 by Tyndale Charitable Trust. Used by permission of Tyndale House Publishers.

On Assignment Publishing Company
www.OnAssignmentPublishing.com

On Assignment Publishing books are available in bookstores everywhere, and on the Web at www.Amazon.com

Endorsements

Many of us long to know how we might rise above our daily challenges and live a life of godliness enjoying all God has for us. Sarah Goebel shares the God-given wisdom that provides insights and practical tools for doing just that.

–Linda Olson, Professional Speaker
Author of *Exceeding your Expectations*
www.madeforsomethingmore.com

In God's holy word, two paths are clearly described for us to follow. The broad path is full of temporary pleasure but ultimately leads to death and distance from the Lord. However, the narrow path is difficult, not chosen by the majority but leads to the joyous love and redemption of His arms, vision, and purpose. In Sarah Goebel's new book, <u>Experience Godliness God's Way</u>, that narrow path is beautifully exemplified through the journey of realizing God's best for us versus the crumbs that we often accept from His table. Sarah helps us to breathe in God's heart for us as His children and His desire for us to be and have all that He has created us for. You will be blessed, encouraged and inspired by this book.

–Charlotte D. Hunt
Speaker, teacher, counselor, and author of
Damaged Goods: An Autobiography

(more endorsements on back cover)

Dedications and Appreciations

I dedicate this book to my grandson Alex Gill, whom I love from my heart. May you grow in your knowledge and understanding of God. May you experience a life of godliness found in an intimate relationship with God. May you have His favor all the days of your life.

I also dedicate this book to all those who desire to reflect Christ's image through their lives that others may come to know Christ. May you experience godliness and contentment which results in an abundant life.

I thank my husband for his unwavering love and support for me to share the gospel of Christ in writing and speaking opportunities. Thank you, Jon, for being a godly man who walks in wisdom, love and grace. Thank you for protecting, encouraging and caring for me. You are my best friend.

I thank my Lord and God, Jesus Christ for pulling me out of the mire and setting my feet upon the rock. Thank you for your unfailing love and long-suffering towards me as I walk, fall down and get back up. You are always here for me no matter what. I love you and pray that you are glorified through all that I say and do as I continue my journey of transformation with you!

Table of Contents

Introduction 9

Chapter One: Where to Find Happiness 13

Chapter Two: Catching God's Vision for Perfection................. 23

Chapter Three: The Gospel of Jesus Christ:
  Empowered for Godliness.. 41

Chapter Four: Discovering the Blessing in Godly Attitudes..... 55

Chapter Five: On With the New – Off With the Old 69

Chapter Six: Happy are the Poor in Spirit 75

Chapter Seven: Happy Are Those Who Mourn 87

Chapter Eight: Meekness Leads to Rest 97

Chapter Nine: Hunger and Thirst for Right Standing
  with God – and Be Satisfied 109

Chapter Ten: The One Who Cares is Cared For 117

Chapter Eleven: Cultivating a Passion for Purity 127

Chapter Twelve: Sons of God 139

Chapter Thirteen: Happy and Favored While
  in the Midst of Persecution 155

Chapter Fourteen: In Summary 165

A Final Thought 175

Appendix A - Godliness Acrostic 177

Appendix B - How to Be Saved 179

Appendix C - Identity Scriptures 183

Endnotes 187

Introduction

But seek first the Kingdom of God and His righteousness…
–Matthew 6:33 NKJV

1 Timothy 6:6 declares, *Godliness with contentment is great gain* (abundance). Christians talk about the abundant life. Yet without a pursuit of God and a desire to walk uprightly before Him, genuine contentment and true blessed living are not available. Matthew 6:33 implores us, *But seek first his kingdom and his righteousness, and all these things will be given to you as well.* This is the pathway to abundance—seeking God and seeking to walk uprightly before Him. You may be in the Kingdom of God, but my question to you is, "Are you seeking His righteousness?" Yes, from a legal standpoint, you have been clothed in the righteousness of Christ. Christ has given you His righteousness as a born-again child of God. But are you committed to living right, according to God's ideas of right living? Are you committed to the practice of the spiritual disciplines and walking uprightly before Him? Are you pursuing godliness?

After receiving salvation, our main goal should be pursuing godliness—becoming like Christ. Why? Simply put, because it is God's main goal for us. My friends, this requires vision, effort and believing in the ability the Scripture says we have in Christ to attain perfection. Jesus claimed in John 10:10 that He came to make an abundant life available for us, and then He shows us the way to it. The way is through perfection or godliness. Unlike many in the church, I believe we can experience the virtue of godliness, add to it contentment and experience a life of great gain (abundance), as declared in 1 Timothy 6:6. I believe it because the Word says it.

Look at these Scriptures:

> *Be perfect, therefore, as your heavenly Father is perfect.*
> –Matthew 5:48

> *Perseverance must finish its work so that you may be mature and complete, not lacking anything.*
> –James 1:4

> *Since we have these promises, dear friends, let us purify ourselves from everything that contaminates body and spirit, perfecting.*
> –2 Corinthians 7:1

> *Let us go on unto perfection.*
> –Hebrews 6:1 KJV

When I read the letters of Paul and Peter, I am again "encouraged" and "commanded" to expect to mature in Christ.

> *Having therefore these promises, dearly beloved, let us cleanse ourselves from all filthiness of the flesh and spirit, perfecting holiness in the fear of God.*
> –2 Corinthians 7:1 KJV

> *Everyone who confesses the name of the Lord must turn away from wickedness.*
> –2 Timothy 2:19b

> *...make every effort to be found spotless, blameless and at peace with him.*
> –2 Peter 3:14

In this book, I hope to inspire you to set your eyes on Christ and make it your personal goal and pursuit to become a reflection of the Holy One—to seek first the kingdom of God and upright living before Him. This is where the life of abundance is found. This is where the blessed life described in the beatitudes exists—a life that is *happy, to be envied, and spiritually prosperous—with life-joy and satisfaction in God's favor and salvation, regardless of outward conditions* (Matthew 5 AMP). Godliness is the pathway to blessedness.

Experiencing godliness is a journey and, therefore, requires commitment, if we are to persevere. It is not a fixed goal that we reach and then can rest to no longer pursue. When Christians abandon the pursuit, they find themselves losing ground in their spiritual walk and fellowship with God. If one never begins the pursuit, the life Christ came to give this side of heaven is forfeited, never to be experienced in fullness while on the earth.

Pursuing a life lived in the Kingdom, and one lived uprightly before God, is an ongoing lifestyle and commitment to grow in Christ. It requires intentional living. It is a lifestyle of choosing to lay aside our fleshly desires and choosing to do what is right before God. Pursuing righteousness is the way of godliness. As we embark on this study, we will consider what true happiness and blessed living look like, and how godliness is the vehicle to experience it. It is my hope that at the end of this study, you will have discovered vision, inspiration and strength for godly living.

If you are not a born-again child of God, you will find that, on your own, you cannot walk in godliness nor discover genuine, lasting happiness. You must have the person of the Holy Spirit dwelling in you. It is He who empowers us to change and grow. For this supernatural indwelling to take place, you must first receive Jesus Christ as your Lord and Savior. If you would like to learn more about how to become a Christian, or if you need to be reassured of your relationship with Christ, please turn to Appendix A at the back of this book at any time while reading. God is waiting for you.

At the end of each chapter you will find a promised blessing, the requirement for the blessing, chapter summary points and questions designed to help you go deeper in reflection, application and growth.

The book may be read without participating in the chapter reflection section, however, you will get more from this study if you will take the time to think about your life and how to practically apply the knowledge and principles illuminated here.

Open your heart to allow the Holy Spirit to reveal to you areas where you may need to change. Just as a hot coal pressed against Isaiah's lips must have resulted in pain, you may experience pain as a realization of your sin surfaces (Isaiah 6:5-8). However, don't get into condemnation. Be sorrowful and repentant. Make a decision to change in the power of the Holy Spirit. Don't forget to rely on His strength. Surrender to Him and He will guide and empower you. Then leave it behind and move forward walking in godliness.

As you read, may you be inspired to commit to a pursuit of godliness, and thereby discover blessedness and great gain. May the Holy Spirit guide you and transform you into a vessel that reflects the image of Christ.

In Christ's Love and For His Glory,

Sarah

Train yourself to be godly. For physical training is of some value, but godliness has value for all things, holding promise for both the present life and the life to come.

–1 Timothy 4:7-8

Chapter One

Where to Find Happiness

Everyone desires to be happy but for many, happiness appears to be elusive. The problem lies in where we are looking to find happiness. Or should I say, it lies in where we fail to look for it.

Before embarking on our study of godliness, I want to mention that there are two kinds of happiness. One is the feeling we have that results from pleasant circumstances and a trouble-free life. However, jobs are lost, people betray us, trophies grow dusty—circumstances change. What happens to our happiness then? It evaporates, as does the dew on a spring morning.

But there is a genuine, lasting happiness that is not dependent on external circumstances. This kind of happiness only comes from God, and it is available to those who live for Him. We get more insight into this as we study the Beatitudes in Matthew Chapter 5. Here Jesus shows us the way to genuine happiness. He begins each beatitude with the word "blessed." The Amplified Version of the New Testament defines blessed as *happy, to be envied, and spiritually prosperous…with life-joy and satisfaction…* Even with this amplification, I do not think we have the depth of the meaning of blessedness that Jesus spoke of in these verses. Nonetheless, we can see that wrapped up in a godly character is where we find the deepest kind of happiness. We will be taking a closer look at each of the beatitudes later in this book. For now, I want you to see that this supernatural, lasting happiness, not contingent on anything except a relationship with God and upright living, is available.

God wants to see us happy. Psalm 35:27 states, *He delights in the well-being of his servant.* In fact, from the very beginning in the Book of Genesis, we see God's desire to bless man. He made a bountiful creation and declared it good. Then He generously gave dominion over the earth to Adam. Because man was sinless, God Himself communed with man, their relationship unhindered by any man-made barrier attempting to cover sin and shame. You see, humans were created for godliness. Sinfulness is not the natural state of man. Godliness is. Sinfulness is the result of the fallen nature of man, but godliness is what we were created for. Christ came to restore that condition within us.

In the beginning, man was created to reflect the glory of God. It was in the purity of their original nature as created by God—a godly nature—that enabled Adam and Eve to experience harmony with God and, therefore, experience happiness. You see, happiness is hidden in godliness. Man's glorious relationship with His Creator was temporarily lost after the fall, as the nature of man from then on was corrupt with sin. However, God's desire and purpose for man never changed. God had a plan to redeem man through His Son, Jesus Christ, and to restore what was lost. He had a plan to sanctify man and make him holy. He had a plan to bless him abundantly and transform him into the godly image of His Son. His plan is being played out in our lives upon the earth.

We see in the Old Testament how God chose Abraham. Through him, he would grow a nation from which He would bring forth His Son the Messiah, to deliver man from judgment and the bondage of sin. God called Abraham and set him apart for His divine purposes. He then grew a nation and called it Israel. God set apart this nation, the descendants of Abraham and Sarah, as His possession; then He set about to make them holy. In Genesis 12:2 NASB, God says to Abram, *And I will make you a great nation, And I will bless you, And make your name great; And so you shall be a blessing.* He then reiterates this promise to Abraham's descendants Isaac and Jacob. In the New Testament speaking to the church, we read in Galatians 3:29: *And if you belong to Christ, then you are Abraham's descendants, heirs according to promise.* As a Christian, you have been set apart to be blessed and to bless others, as was Abraham. You have also been set apart that the Messiah may be revealed through you individually. The church is set apart corporately for this revelation of Christ, just as Christ was revealed through the nation of Israel by being born into the world through it.

In the book of Exodus and Leviticus, we see God setting things apart for His purpose and use and calling them holy. For example, God declared 'holy,' each article used in the tabernacle structure and furnishings. He then proceeded to instruct the Israelites to cleanse what He called holy, making it pure and holy in practice (Exodus 40:9-10). We see God choosing Aaron to be a priest to Himself in Exodus 40:12-13. He chose him, cleansed him and commanded the garments He had declared holy be put on him. God conferred holiness upon a person or item. If God declared it holy, then it was holy and set apart for His purpose and use.

God's practice of conferring holiness upon people and things continues to present day. As a Christian, God chose you, set you apart and has declared you holy. He has set you apart to grow in godliness. He has sanctified you, cleansing you by the blood of Jesus Christ; and He continues to sanctify you, as He transforms you into the image of His holy Son. The more we experience Christ's nature, the more blessed we are.

> *God had a plan to redeem man through His Son, Jesus Christ, and to restore what was lost.*

The blessings God promised Abraham belong to us as Abraham's heirs through faith in Christ. Yet there is so much more for the Christian than what Abraham had available to him. We are heirs of God in Christ Jesus. When Christ ascended, He sent the Holy Spirit to dwell within His purchased possession, to complete this work of perfection in us. It is His priority goal for our lives that we be transformed as a reflection of Christ (Romans 8:29). Everyone who receives Christ as their Lord and Savior has been set apart for transformation. They have been set apart for blessedness, godliness and communion with God—a life of great gain.

1 Peter 2:9 MSG, *But you are chosen by God, chosen for the high calling of priestly work, chosen to be a holy people, God's instruments to do his work and speak out for him, to tell others of the night-and-day difference he made for you.* If you are chosen and called by God, then you are called to be holy. God has given you a new heart, one that desires Him and desires holiness (Ezekiel 36:26-27). He is now working this holiness out in your life. You may ask, why is it some Christians do not seem to live any different than

others in the world? It has to do with our willingness to surrender to the plans of God for our life. We progress to the degree we give Him the rule over our thoughts, will, emotions and events. Please do not miss this. It is to the degree we release control of our lives to Christ that we reflect His image through our lives. His spirit empowers us. His kingship guarantees we will reach our goal.

Jesus Christ made the abundant life available when He defeated all sin and authority that was contrary to God. The availability of this blessed, happy life is a gift to all who call upon His name. But it is experienced as we walk in godliness.

Some mistakenly think that when Scripture speaks of our walking in godliness that it is talking about perfection as though we can be "supremely perfect" as is God. According to <u>Vines Dictionary,</u> godliness "denotes that piety which, characterized by a God-ward attitude, does that which is well-pleasing to Him."[1] Therefore, walking in godliness doesn't mean you never have a bad thought cross your mind. It doesn't mean you never have a feeling of rejection or aggravation. You can have a holy walk and still have a bad-hair day. As we will discuss in a future chapter, this kind of erroneous teaching about our pursuit of godliness has caused some to either become sanctimoniously religious or to give up altogether, upon the realization that they are not able to accomplish such perfection. The truth is, only one man has ever walked, or will ever walk, in supreme perfection; and that One is the Lord Jesus Christ. And the Bible says even He experienced temptation. But please understand that it is crucial for believers to have a vision of Christ's holiness and of Christ living in and through them. With a vision of Christ living in you and perfection being attained through His power instead of your own, perfection becomes a desirable goal that you can move toward.

You see, without vision, God's people perish. In other words, they fail to experience the life God has planned for them. It is imperative that we get a biblical vision of godliness for our lives and the blessings that come with it. It is crucial that we believe that it is attainable or we will fail to train ourselves in it. 1Timothy 4:7-8, *Train yourself to be godly. For physical training is of some value, but godliness has value for all things, holding promise for both the present life and the life to come.*

Using the analogy of the physical training, which disciplined athletes participate in when preparing for competition, Paul is urging Timothy to enter into a vigorous training program for His spiritual formation. Since he is imploring him to train himself to be godly, then godliness must be a goal that we can reach. He is telling us it is attainable if we will train ourselves and that it is more valuable than anything else we can have or do. Just as athletes have their visual and physical barriers to overcome, we as spiritual athletes have obstacles to conquer as well. And just as the athlete must be committed to a "quitting is not an option" mentality, so must we be devoted to an intensive training program and see it through to the finish line. That finish line is where we meet Christ face to face, either by death or His second coming. Without vision—without believing we can attain godliness—we don't bother committing to this kind of discipline. Therefore, we fail to overcome the challenges. We must do our part, while surrendering to the person of the Holy Spirit. He then diligently works to change us.

It is so beautiful how the Holy Spirit shines His light in the cracks and crevices of our heart and the depths of our soul, where no one but He sees. He reveals to us these needed areas of change. We then choose to partner with Him in this process of changing our attitudes. When we get a vision of who we are not and who we are becoming in Christ, we are empowered to surrender these areas, instead of justifying them. With vision, we welcome His beacon light and we are ready to change. However, without a belief that we can attain godliness, we unconsciously think, "Why even try?" On the other hand, when we believe we can experience it, we begin to stand on the promise that He will supernaturally perfect us. We become like King David and surrender, saying, *Create in me a clean heart Oh God. Renew a right spirit within me* (Psalm 51:10). And we expect that He will. Our faith for change is seen in our actions as we begin to spend the necessary time with God in prayer, and in His Word, which is required to produce change.

1Timothy 6:6, *Godliness with contentment is great gain*, emphasizes the importance of where we set our vision. It also emphasizes the results of our attitude towards God. The one who fears the Lord and pursues a growing relationship with God will walk increasingly in blessedness. He will increasingly experience happiness as he increasingly experiences godliness. This is the Christian's race. It is not against one another, but is our personal race to conform to the image of Christ. This is conformity to godliness or perfection. This is what life is about. So much of the church has looked beyond this foundational principle, trying to accomplish the work of Christ in the world while bypassing this much needed work that starts within our individual souls. The result is Christian leaders, who are unsanctified in regards to practical holiness. This affects their intimacy with God and their attitudes as well as their behavior in the way they deal with other members of the body of Christ; behavior that, unfortunately, sometimes hurts people and causes them to turn away from the church. We can help eliminate this problem, simply by accepting the challenge and responsibility of our personal spiritual training and formation.

How do we grow spiritually? How are we to be changed from looking like a sinner to looking like Christ? We are exhorted in 2 Peter 3:18 to grow in grace and knowledge of Jesus Christ. *But grow in the grace and knowledge of our Lord and Savior Jesus Christ. To him be glory both now and forever! Amen.* This means we have to spend time in the Bible and prayer.

There are so many things that distract us from our devotion to God and the study of His Word. We are distracted by the busyness of life. We are distracted by the children, the grocery shopping, our jobs and families. We are distracted by ministry, our friendships and conflicts, as well as our challenges, trials and tribulations. If we do not keep our focus in check, our health and financial challenges can consume our attention, leaving no room for God. When you have devotion towards God, it will show itself in your walk with Him through the things you choose to do or choose NOT to do. In other words, your choices are a reflection of your reverence and fear of God. A life where the choices and decisions concerning time, activities, money, and other resources continually contradict the ways of God, cannot—will not—lead one to find happiness. On the other hand, a lifestyle that regularly, even if not perfectly, reflects devotion towards God will accordingly enjoy genuine happiness and lasting contentment.

Colossians 3:1 commands us to focus our attention on Christ who sits in the heavenlies. He lives above the things of the world, undaunted by them. As Christians, we must live intentional lives focused on a higher realm – the Kingdom of God. We need to ask, "What is God doing and what is God saying in the situations of life?"

The second part of 2 Peter 3:18 gives us the MOST important concept we must get in understanding and experiencing spiritual formation. The KEY we find in this verse is GIVING THE GLORY TO GOD. This is vital in making progress into Christ-likeness.

As we spend time in the Word of God and in prayer communing with God, His thoughts will naturally become our thoughts, and our perspectives will begin to line up with His. This God-ward focus results in transforming every aspect of our lives. Our attitudes are transformed as our desire to conform increases, and we are changed from the inside out. We will discuss this important part of our walk and transformation in a later chapter. For now, I will leave it that, without devotion to God, one may have some moments or days of temporary and fleeting happiness; however, genuine happiness, not subject to change due to exterior circumstances, is only available to those who intentionally devote and focus their lives on God and His glory.

The blessed life is not without cost. We see in the Old Testament that the blessings come along with an "if." The lesson in the Book of Judges, as well as many other books, is that conformity to the law of God brings prosperity, whereas apostasy leads to captivity. In the New Testament, we see that the supremely blessed life is available because of the death, resurrection and ascension of Christ. Believers experience a "mystical union" with Christ. His Spirit dwelling within us empowers us to live a godly life, while conforming to His image. When we surrender our attitudes to His Lordship, we begin to experience godliness. This sanctification of our lives is developed through our cooperation with, and in the power of, the Holy Spirit, Who comforts, strengthens, guides and transforms us.

The Bible tells us that God is with us and will never leave us nor forsake us. No matter how low or how high we are, God is just a glimpse away. Our sensitivity to His presence increases when we practice His presence in our lives. And as we experience His presence, we become more committed to change.

The Blessing: Empowerment for godly living – Hope of attaining perfection, happiness and abundant living

The Recipient: Believers in Christ who have received the knowledge that Christ dwells in them

...the mystery which has been hidden from the past ages and generations, but has now been manifested to His saints, to whom God willed to make known what is the riches of the glory of this mystery among the Gentiles, which is **Christ in you, the hope of glory.**

–Col 1:26-27

Reflect and Grow:

Things to Remember:

- Happiness is hidden in godliness and Christ's life lived through ours.
- Surrender to Christ to Reflect Christ.
- Conformation is empowered by the Holy Spirit – Transformation is guaranteed by Christ's Kingship.
- The Christians' race is one of conformity to the image of Christ.
- God's most important goal for our lives is our transformation into the image of Christ.
- A life reflecting devotion to God is a life walking in godliness.
- To progress toward godliness, we must increase in grace and a knowledge of Christ.

Seek and Apply:

1. Think about this Scripture - *Seek first the Kingdom of God and His righteousness, and then all these things will be added unto you* (Matthew 6:33). What is meant by "all these things"?

2. Again, looking at Matthew 6:33, what does it mean to you to *seek first the Kingdom of God?* What is this kingdom? How can we seek for it? Why do we need to do this in order to experience happiness? In order to experience godliness?

3. Looking at the same Scripture, what does it mean to seek God's righteousness? Why do we need to seek God's righteousness in order to experience happiness? In order to experience godliness?

4. What examples were in your life this week that witness your attitude is to keep God and His priorities as your first priority? What examples show this attitude as a general rule?

5. Read Isaiah 55:1, 2. If Isaiah were living today, he would be asking, "Are you happy with your life?" When Isaiah asked this of the Israelites knowing the answer was 'no,' he then proceeded to answer the question, instructing them how to find a more satisfying life. In your own words, what was he telling them they should stop doing? What was he telling them they should do instead? How does this speak to your personal life?

6. What will it cost you to walk in godliness? What will you gain? Is it worth it to you?

7. Think about your daily responsibilities, e.g., washing dishes, job, children, relationships, etc. Is God at the center of your life – your activities? Is He on your mind while living life? Why do you think this is true for your life?

8. Is there any area of your life where you have **not** released control and allowed Christ His rightful Lordship? What is in His place? What can you do to change this?

9. Do you think about God in the good times? Bad times? What can you do to intentionally make yourself more aware of His presence and bring your thoughts to Him more often?

10. What is meant by the phrase "God sets apart"?

11. God has set us apart for His purpose. What is His goal for us according to Romans 8:29?

12. You are holy because God _____ you holy. You are _____ in holiness to the degree that you are _____ to the working of the Holy Spirit in your life.

13. A godly life is one that, although perhaps not perfectly, does regularly reflect devotion towards God. What does a life look like that reflects devotion to God?

Father, I thank You to reveal Yourself to me, Your character and glory. I ask You to give me a vision of conforming my life to line up with Your ways, while You transform me from the inside out into Your image. I thank You for setting me apart, calling me holy and empowering me with the Holy Spirit's abiding presence to be all that You have called me to be. It is Christ in me that is my hope of glory. In His name, Amen.

For those whom He foreknew [of whom He was aware and loved beforehand], He also destined from the beginning [foreordaining them] to be molded into the image of His Son [and share inwardly His likeness], that He might become the firstborn among many brethren.

—Romans 8:29 AMP

Chapter Two

Catching God's Vision for Perfection

Most of us are diligent in our pursuit of being the best we can be in our jobs, hobbies, entertainment and education. Humans are naturally goal-oriented, and if God's goal for perfection is not our own goal, we will default to self-centered objectives and idolatry. For example, we spend an excessive amount of our time, energy and money to perfect our bodies and gain possessions. We might work hard to participate in sporting events with an expectation to receive the prize. These activities may be harmless and may even profit our bodies, but if they are a goal that is holding priority above the goal to attain perfection in Christ, it is idolatrous behavior. Without godliness as our priority goal, we will find ourselves in idolatry, putting our selfish objectives before God's. Mark 8:36 KJV says, *For what shall it profit a man, if he shall gain the whole world, and lose his own soul?* You can work hard at accomplishing many things and you might even find some pleasure in it, yet that pleasure will be hollow and empty if your priorities are out of order. Following Jesus and pursuing His goals is the only pathway to the genuine, abundant life. And God's priority goal for us is clear. *For those whom He foreknew [of whom He was aware and loved beforehand], He also destined from the beginning [foreordaining them] to be molded into the image of His Son [and share inwardly His likeness], that He might become the firstborn among many brethren,* Romans 8:29 AMP. God will stop at nothing, but will work all things in our lives together for His purpose of forming us into the image of His Son, Jesus Christ. Many, however, have lost a clear vision of Christ, His power and His goal for our lives. It has been lost in the lie, "You cannot be perfect so why try?" For the unregenerate, this is true. But for those who have Christ dwelling in them, they have everything they need to reach the goal of living a godly and upright life. Christ in us is our hope of glory.

In the introduction, I shared Scriptures in which God commands us, as new creations in Christ, to be perfect. Would God command us to do anything that is unattainable? Of course, He wouldn't. The problem we have in accepting that it is God's will for us to set this goal for our lives—a goal of godliness on this side of heaven—is that our idea of godliness is different than God's.

We also have a false notion concerning the way to live in godliness. God's way is that we mature into devoted disciples of Christ who are healed, fruitful and influential by getting a vision of Christ and seeing ourselves becoming like Him. His way is that we trust Him to empower us to conform while He transforms us from inside out. His way is to call every stage of our development perfect, from the sowing of the (perfect) seed to it's maturity where Christ-like is what we have become in our actions. This does not mean that we don't have work to do ourselves. Scripture tells us that faith without works is dead. As we will discuss in a future chapter, we must be diligent to sow the Word into our lives. There is no self-reliance involved either. We are ever conscious and dependent on the Holy Spirit for insight and conviction, strength, comfort and growth. God's idea is that we set our eyes on Him and thereby be changed. *But we all, with unveiled face, beholding as in a mirror the glory of the Lord, are being transformed into the same image from glory to glory, just as from the Lord, the Spirit* (2 Corinthians 3:18).

Michael W. H. Holcomb in his book, <u>Attainable Perfection</u>, lists some **wrong ideas** people have concerning perfection. They include:

"Having an ideal past

Having no quirks, weaknesses, or blind spots

Being incapable of making a mistake

Being beyond criticism, embarrassment or frustration

Never being vulnerable

Never having setbacks or regrets

Having the best of all character traits

Possessing unbreakable, unbeatable will power

Always having a great day

Always feeling good about yourself

Always being right"[2]

These ideas are not God's thoughts concerning perfection – quite the opposite. Godly perfection is attained in cooperation with the promptings and power of the Holy Spirit at work in our lives. Whereas, the goals listed above indicate an unrealistic assumption that we can evolve into someone who needs nothing or no one. This is the same deception Eve fell to. Adam and Eve were perfect until they ate from the forbidden tree in an attempt to become like God—no longer dependent on God as His creation. Thus, the godly are quick to acknowledge their reliance on God. Striving for perfection in our own strength and power will not result in permanent change. It will instead result in defeat by exhaustion. We must have the power and hand of God shaping and forming us and we must recognize that we will always need God in order to maintain a state of perfection.

Holcomb also shares another interesting list of ideas concerning perfection. These ideas are held by the sanctimonious Christian and create a religious atmosphere where people are doomed to fail. Their failure then results in perpetuating the lie to themselves and others that no one can walk in perfection—no one can experience godliness. After all, they tried and failed. This line of thought produces behavior that denies the power of God available to work in our lives to perfect us. Take a look at these ideas:

Being perfect means reaching a stage where one…

"Is never tempted

Never makes an oversight in his walk

Always has feelings of brotherly love, divine grace, supernatural movement, and the like

Is automatically motivated to perform godly duties such as prayer, witnessing, and going to church

Is so heavenly minded, he can go without modern creature comforts and get by with the most basic bare essentials

> Is so spiritually minded, he can successfully abstain from sensations like excitement, recreation, or even passion.
>
> Has finally overcome all personal quirks and self-perceived obstacles (internal and external)
>
> Has gone beyond pain, lack, weakness, and commonality to attain uninterrupted tranquility of the soul."[3]

Some people may have a form of godliness, but lack the power of true, genuine change. They are more concerned about exterior actions and what people think, than they are about doing what is necessary to be truly transformed from the inside out into the image of Christ. These people go to church, know Christianese (all the right things to say) and all the right things are done to look good, but genuine attitudes of belief, love and worship are lacking. These are the Christians (whether pretend or real, only God knows) who will do everything in their power to put you down so that they may build themselves up. They also tend to be the judgmental people who will insist you are the same person you were ten years ago, denying the power of God to change lives. There is no second chance with these folks. Timothy says these are they who are *holding to a form of godliness, although they have denied its power; Avoid such men as these...* (2 Timothy 3-5). We not only want to avoid them, but we want to examine ourselves for like behavior and if it exists, repent and begin living in the power of truth.

Religious tradition always neutralizes the power of the Word of God. Still some people are drawn to it for various reasons, although it is beyond me why. I suppose it is just simple deception and the effects of the fall. We will save that discussion for another book. For now, understand that the majority of people end up rebelling against such nonsense.

For the most part, in addition to rebellion, I have noticed that much of this type of thinking in the church has resulted in an almost dog-eat-dog kind of atmosphere, where people are striving to climb the ladder of position, whether it be a realized position in the church hierarchy or a perceived position through relationship with those in the church hierarchy. These misled souls wrongly equate this to a witness of their own spirituality; and sadly, others, who are looking up the ladder, see them as walking closer to God as well. Many times the opposite is true. Many are influenced, having ungodly ways imparted to them through these types of attitudes. These mindsets in the body of Christ have caused much pain in the lives of many, either brought on by their own wrong attitude or due to someone else seeing them as a threat to the position they have carved out for themselves in that particular community of believers. I am sure there are other reasons but this is enough to make my point. The principle of living life on a ladder is practiced in relationship choices as well as choices regarding ministry activities. A system of religious politics is formed within the church and God-seeking Christians, who do not understand it nor know how to function in it, get hurt. Those who know "how to climb the ladder" play the game and put their skills to work to position themselves to reach a level where they may be viewed as "spiritually mature" although they many times are missing the heart of God. It is the same situation as we read about with the Pharisees in the gospels. Jesus spoke in Matthew 6:2 concerning them saying, *So when you give to the poor, do not sound a trumpet before you, as the hypocrites do in the synagogues and in the streets, so that they may be honored by men. Truly I say to you, they have their reward in full.* It is a sad situation when people are so caught up in the political atmosphere in the church that their hearts are closed to aspiring to genuine spiritual maturity. They are more concerned about position and what men think of them in the church than experiencing the oneness in relationship with God that results directly from our focus on Christ and our goal to become like Him.

Without godliness as our priority goal, we will find ourselves in idolatry, putting our selfish objectives before God's.

As leaders within the body of Christ, we need to lead people away from living their life with a ladder mentality. We can start by becoming more conscientious to set aside our difference of opinions and personalities and be diligent to not allow differences to influence us towards showing favoritism or disqualifying individuals for Kingdom work. For this to happen is a very sad thing; and although God still sets on the throne and allows it for His purposes, it still saddens His heart. In my experiences, I have concluded that this is an issue existing more with women than men. I pray that women within the church will surrender their desire to control and allow God to bring forth His ministry through the sisters in Christ He has gifted for His purpose. There is room for multiple personalities and giftings in the body of Christ within the local church and various church networks.

It truly saddens my heart, but it is true. Just like people in the world are climbing the ladder of success, we see many people in the Kingdom approaching their church life and spiritual development on a ladder. They strive to reach the rung of permanent, self-reliant status through their relationships with "so and so," or their "good works," as well as unhealthy "busyness" in the church, when the only true pathway for spiritual growth is spending time with God and surrendering their lives to Him. The status that is associated with the ladder pattern of growth can become an area of pride and stunt true spiritual growth and intimacy with God. Life on a ladder also produces envy, feelings of superiority for those on the higher rung, and inferiority for those who are looking up at them. Perhaps the most serious flaw of this idea is the sense of failure that it perpetuates. When you are on a higher rung and slip, you begin to feel like you have failed and can never reach that level again. You begin to see yourself as less than others who appear to be moving forward and upward while you are on your way down. In other words, this false idea of perfection begins to appear unreachable.

Life lived according to God's plan is different. God views human development like a garden. God has made you perfect in Christ. You sow and weed the garden and then you reap what you have sown. This is how you become and maintain perfection status. When you mess up, you are able to repent of your sin, be cleansed and receive forgiveness (1 John 1:9). There is no striving or elitism in this model. There is a time of sowing, watering and reaping. There are seasons and time for growth.

Many different kinds of plants are being grown in the garden of our lives and we harvest multiple crops of these plants. We know these as the fruit of the Spirit (Galatians 5:22). Our responsibility is to keep the soil fertile and to keep the garden rid of weeds (ungodly attitudes) that would prevent the good fruit from coming forth. In the garden paradigm for human development, we are free to help one another succeed in our spiritual formation, as well as in our individual assignments from God. We are free to add nourishment for one another's growth, instead of the poison of gossip, envy and strife. After all, each life is a garden within the Kingdom where the Son is at the center, rather than an organization with a ladder as its center, where there is only room for a few people on a rung at a time. Well, they may have God at the center, but they have Him at the top of the ladder with the ladder being the only way to reach Him.

I hope you are beginning to see that God's idea of human development is not a picture of a ladder where one climbs to a higher rank. His idea is simple. We see the simplicity of it in all of creation. We are of the earth, formed from the dust of the ground, and our lives flow and grow in unison with the rest of the earth. Think about it. God refers to His people *as the planting of the Lord* in Isaiah 61:3. Humans begin as a seed in their mother's womb. They grow in the womb as a seed grows in the fertile soil, carrying within itself like seed to reproduce after itself. Humans are then born onto the earth and they are nurtured, grow and bear fruit, according to what they sow in their lives. God speaks of our having seasons in our lives, and He speaks of planting and replanting, uprooting and pruning, grafting and watering. All of these activities are done in a garden, not on a ladder.

Then there is the parable of the sower, found in Luke 8. In verse 11 we read, *Now the parable is this: the seed is the word of God.* This is the simplicity of God. The seed we should be sowing into our lives is the Word of God. The more time we spend reading and speaking the Word of God, the more seed we are planting into our lives that has within itself the character of Jesus. In John 1:1,14 we read that Jesus is the Word who became flesh and dwelt among us. The Word of God is Jesus. When you read and speak the written Word of God, you are sowing Jesus, His character and His power into your life. Because seed reproduces after itself, as we sow Jesus (the Word – the Seed), Jesus is going to be what we produce in our own life. It is all about the seed—Jesus! It is about sowing the seed, the Word of God, Jesus Christ, into the garden of our own lives, and then He is reproduced in our lives. Herein lies our pathway to godliness—sowing the seed which is the Word of God, Jesus. Religious ideas have complicated the simple message and pathway God has shown us to spiritual maturity. Instead of striving to climb a ladder, we are to live a simple life of sowing and reaping.

> *If you have godly attitudes, then your life will produce godly behavior.*

The great commission of sharing the gospel of Christ will also become a natural thing for those who think like Christ, because evangelism is His heart. It is the character of the seed that is growing within us. Christ desires to reach and transform into his image, all of whom the Father has given Him. As people become like Christ, they begin to worship God and He is glorified. This is the very heart of missions.

God determined perfection to be attained by sowing the Word of God into our lives and watering it with prayer. The weeds are uprooted as we sow God's Seed. This is God's way for us to experience godliness—to live a life devoted to God, sowing and reaping Christ. A life devoted to God will embrace obedience of His commands, guard the garden of life and reproduce the likeness of Christ through it..

It is imperative to understand that perfection or godliness is not living a life where we never need to sow. If that were possible, we would be at a place of not needing God. God's idea of perfection for us includes dependence upon Him. This means we rely on the Word of God. As previously mentioned, when Adam and Eve walked in perfection before the fall, they walked dependent on God and kept his word. It is when the serpent deceived Eve into thinking that if she would disobey God and eat the fruit from the tree God had commanded them to refrain from, that she would be like God instead of dependent on God, that perfection was lost. To be perfect as God commands us to be perfect, requires that we surrender our self reliance and depend on Him. We must sow the Seed (Christ – the Word of God) into our lives in order to experience transformation, and we must be diligent to guard our lives by keeping our life free of sin. This kind of devotion requires effort. As the Holy Spirit produces the fruit from the seed we have sown, God sees every stage of growth as "perfect."

As we sow the Word, we produce Jesus. We pull up the evil thoughts and desires, as the Holy Spirit reveals them with the sowing of the Word. Therefore, perfection is not something we can do on our own, nor is it something we reach, as though we have reached the top of the ladder. It is not something attained where we can say, "I have conquered that. Now I am finished with it." It is, instead, an ongoing process. Like the garden, we have to care for it. Weeds will spring up again and again. But each time, we have the opportunity to plant, water and harvest the likeness of Christ. This is God's idea of godliness.

We will always need God. Without interaction with Him, in prayer and through the written Word, there is no devotion to Him. You cannot seek the Kingdom of God and His righteousness and at the same time live a prayerless life, void of the Word of God. Without inviting God's participation in our lives, the world's ideas and philosophies and the cares and trials of life will overtake us, leaving the image of Christ unseen in our lives.

Another sad consequence of the ladder mentality has been seen in the moral failure of our spiritual leaders. Some built a ladder in their hearts and saw themselves on the top rung. They failed to keep the garden of life free of weeds (sin), due to a false belief that they had attained a spiritual level of growth, where they could relax in their gardening. The weeds took over and they moved from a state of perfection to imperfection.[4]

You cannot maintain a healthy, growing garden without spending time sowing the seed, watering, and weeding that which doesn't belong there. Without sowing the Word, you cannot reap the Word in your life. When you begin to think that you can maintain godliness without a continual sowing of Seed, it won't be long and you will fall off that ladder you have built in your heart. However, I do want to stress that if that has happened to you, God can restore you to an even greater place than you once were. He can bring you into an even greater relationship with Him. God so desires us to be perfect that He has given us a way to instantly return to perfection and start moving in the right direction again. When a weed takes root, a true repentant heart, receipt of God's forgiveness and sowing the Word of Truth will uproot it and return us to a state of perfection (1 John 1:9). We replace the weed by sowing the Word in its place. Depending on the situation, of course, that doesn't mean that there will not be uncomfortable consequences of the sin to remain in our lives. To reap godliness, requires continual sowing of godly seed that produces after its kind.

Please understand that there will be many times we will have to produce the same kind of harvest we produced in the past. For example, you may have struggled with forgiving someone who hurt you. If you were living out your life on a ladder, when you forgave, you saw yourself as having climbed up a rung, expecting not to have this same kind of trial in life again. Yet you find yourself faced with it again, and so you fall down a rung or two. Feeling like a failure, you dropped down a rung or two on that ladder of success existing in your heart. What anxiety you felt. Finally you released forgiveness and regained your position. This time you were sure you had this challenge of life conquered. Suddenly something happened or someone did something that was even more devastating to your emotions. Did forgiveness come automatically? No, it didn't. So you decided you must be a spiritual failure, questioning, "Why can't I conquer this?" Or, as I use to say, "Why am I going around this mountain again?" We have incorrectly believed we are to reach higher levels when faced with these kind of challenges in life, where we can produce Christ-likeness all on our own. Not so. God has called us to be sowers who will be given opportunities time and time again to plant seeds of Christ and reap multiple harvests of each of His character traits through our lives. Again, God's way of godliness is living dependent on Him, not independent from Him.

We are all equal in Christ with no one living on a higher level than another. All Christians are called to sow Christ into and harvest Christ through their lives. This is God's way of multiplying Christ's presence on the earth.

I hope you are beginning to see the difference between God's way of godliness and the false ideas of godliness we have embraced. We need to quit thinking of our life in terms of levels of maturity, as though we are on a ladder; instead, we should view our life according to the description God has given in His Word. God does not intend for us to live our lives passing grades or levels of success, as though we are in school and will never have to pass that one again. He intends that we will always need Him. Therefore, we all have opportunities to sow the Word for forgiveness, patience, trust, love, kindness, humility, and meekness, many times over in our lifetime. You must sow the seed (the Word – Jesus), water (prayer), and go through the entire process, again, to produce the fruit of Christ-likeness—the opposite fruit of whatever weed (ungodly attitude) is attempting to sprout up in your life. When impatience shows up, uproot it by sowing patience. When fear and distrust show up, sow seeds of love and faith. Your Bible is a seed sack containing every kind of seed you need to uproot any kind of weed and grow in its place spiritual fruit. There is no such thing as conquering these challenges in our lives to the point we will never find ourselves dealing with them again because our life is like a garden. Multiple harvests of the same fruit are produced in your life just as in a healthy garden. Perfection is not reaching another rung of success. Perfection is not a class position. It is an ongoing practice of producing the things of Jesus.[5] Our trials and challenges give us opportunities to produce another crop of love, joy, peace, long-suffering, kindness, goodness, faithfulness, gentleness, and self-control (Galatians 5:22-23). And God looks at us and proclaims, "Perfect" again and again.

Jesus through the Holy Spirit is committed and passionate about bringing us to perfection. He came to save us and to fix us in the here and now. He is always with us, available to empower us to walk upright and godly before Him.

> *Now the God of peace…make you perfect in every good work to do his will, working in you that which is well pleasing in his sight, through Jesus Christ; to whom be glory forever and ever Amen.* –Hebrews 13:20,21
>
> *For it is God which worketh in you both to will and to do of His good pleasure.* –Philippians 2:13 KJV

We can experience godliness, if we will get off the ladder and begin to view life as a garden. If we will get God's vision, believe Him, trust Him, follow Him and rely on Him, we can walk in godliness. The garden pattern for living a life of godliness is doable. Man's idea of perfection with its religious sanctimony—daring people to prove their spirituality by enduring their church disciplines and man-made traditions—is not. Man's way of perfection results in destruction. God's way results in godliness, blessedness, an intimate relationship with God—a life of abundance.

There is also a non-perfection sanctimony in today's contemporary church culture, which is equally as destructive to our pursuit of godliness as sanctimonious perfection. This culture is one where believers proclaim, "If you are really sincere, you will have a church like ours. One that is casual, cool and without rules." I had someone share with me one time that it was the belief of their church that if someone comes to church wearing a cross, then they are religious. My response is that kind of thinking is religious in itself. How can they determine the heart of man? I will continue wearing my cross as it reminds me of the sacrifice Christ made for me. That reminder encourages me to live godly before Him. It reminds me that I have been forgiven and accepted by God. It reminds me of the freedom I now have from sin, because He conquered it. It reminds me that I have power, because He is no longer on the cross, but lives and empowers me. Whether peer-pressured or traditional piety, these kind of attitudes are anemic and artificial, hindering genuine spiritual growth.

> *God's way results in godliness, blessedness, an intimate relationship with God – a life of abundance.*

Both types of sanctimonious fantasies are used by the enemy as distractions, corrupting concepts, harmful ambitions and counterfeit values that lead to frustration and exhaustion for many who are exposed to it. True spirituality and maturity can never be experienced on a ladder of any kind. Freedom and success is found in the unpretentious, simplistic perfection found in Jesus.

We often use Scripture to encourage one another in our life goals and endeavors, saying, "You can do it in Christ." Perhaps instead of using Scripture to support our weakness and propensity to sin, we should use the Word of God and encourage one another in our spiritual goal and command to experience godly perfection. After all, it is God's greatest goal for us, and He instructs us towards this goal. It is doable as we partner with Him.

> *If God be for us, who can be against us?* –Romans 8:31 KJV
>
> *I can do all things through Christ which strengtheneth me.*
> –Philippians 4:13 KJV
>
> *...Greater is he that is in you, than he that is in the world.*
> –1 John 4:4 KJV
>
> *But my God shall supply all your need according to his riches in glory by Christ Jesus.* –Philippians 4:19 KJV

It all begins with believing that if God has commanded us, then it must be available. With faith that "God said it so that settles it," we can envision ourselves attaining it. God said, *Where there is no vision, the people perish* (Proverbs 29:18 KJV). It is imperative that we get vision from the Word. The New Living Translation states it this way, *When people do not accept divine guidance, they run wild.* You must have a vision, if you are to progress towards perfection. In order to get a vision of godliness for our lives, we need to believe in it. As we receive God's Word as Truth, we will begin to see our lives through the eyes of God. We need to look at Christ. As the infinite God-man, He is our example. Reading the gospels, in particular the Gospel of John, is very helpful to us in our understanding of who Christ is and how He lived. We can also look at Paul's life. What a great disciple He was. In his letters to the church, he encourages us to follow him as he followed Christ. Studies on godly character will strengthen our vision.

The Apostle Paul is a great communitarian of the teachings of Jesus. We find his nine-fold commentary on the nine-fold Beatitudes in the spiritual fruit he lists in Galatians 5:22-23. There is a marvelous unity found between the Galatians fruit of the spirit and the teachings of Jesus in the Beatitudes.

Notice that the subject of the first and eighth Beatitude is inheriting the Kingdom of God, as is the subject of the Fruit of the Spirit. Matthew 5:3, *Blessed are the poor in spirit, for theirs is the kingdom of God* and Matthew

5:10, *Blessed are you when you are persecuted for righteousness' sake for you shall inherit the kingdom of God.* Another area of comparison is where we see the lists of the works of the flesh. Paul lists 15 categories (Galatians 19) and Jesus mentions 15 like-categories in the gospels between the lists found in Mark 7:21-22 and Matthew 15:18-19. The difference in these teachings is that Paul is describing not the inner attitudes themselves as Jesus shared, but the consequence of those inner attitudes. The Fruit of the Spirit is the outward manifestation of inward godliness.

The Lord Jesus says, *'Out of the heart'* or out of one's inner attitudes come all these categories of evil. Whereas Paul says, *'The works of the flesh are'* and lists 15 categories of behavior that are a result of those ungodly heart attitudes Christ mentioned. Paul wants his readers to understand what the consequences of evil attitudes will look like in their life.

I want you to see, however, that the nine fruit listed as fruit of the Spirit correspond exactly to the nine beatitudes. When you and I as born-again Christians desire and seek God's righteousness; when we **will** ourselves to have these nine godly inner attitudes seen in Matthew chapter 5, God will correspondingly produce this fruit as seen in Galatians 5. This fruit is our inner attitudes brought to surface. It is the result of thoughts we have meditated on that have formed within us, strongholds that we call attitudes. It is the harvest of what we have sown—the Seed that is The Word of God Who is Jesus.

So the Lord is talking about inner attitudes, *'in the heart.'* Paul is speaking of the **results** of those attitudes in our behavior, *'the works of the flesh.'* Comparing our lives to a tree, the fruit is something that comes forth from inside the tree. The tree is known by the fruit it bears. If your inner attitudes are sinful, then your fruit or works of the flesh will be sinful. If you have godly attitudes, then your life will produce godly behavior. The fruit of the Spirit is produced by the Spirit. It is the work of the Spirit, but the attitudes we allow to live within us are our responsibility. Jesus tells us what thoughts we are to meditate on to form godly attitudes within. He is telling us what to do, so that God can do His work in us. Paul then tells us how those inner attitudes will express themselves in our lives, whether holy or evil attitudes producing either godly or ungodly lifestyles. 2 Corinthians 10:5 tells us that we are to destroy thoughts that enter our minds that oppose the knowledge of God, taking thoughts captive to the obedience of Christ.

Romans 12:2 reiterates that we do have a part in our transformation. It says, *Do not conform any longer to the pattern of this world, but be transformed by the renewing of your mind. Then you will be able to test and approve what God's will is—his good, pleasing and perfect will.* God will be faithful to produce godly fruit through our lives, when we are faithful to do our part by drawing near to Him and living our life faithfully sowing the Seed (the Word—Jesus) and conforming our thoughts to His.

The Blessing: Empowerment for godly living: Enablement to see things through God's eyes

The Recipient: Those chosen to be holy and perform priestly duties; those who receive God's vision for believers to attain perfection through Christ

But you are chosen by God, chosen for the high calling of priestly work, chosen to be a holy people, God's instruments to do his work and speak out for him, to tell others of the night-and-day difference he made for you.
–1 Peter 2:9 MSG

Reflect and Grow:

Things to Remember:

- Instead of striving to climb a ladder to attain spiritual maturity, we are to sow spiritual seeds into the garden of life thereby reaping a harvest of Christ-likeness.

- Perfection is not success as the world sees it. Perfection is not a class position. It is an ongoing practice of producing the things of Jesus through one's devotion to Him.

- The fruit of the spirit is the outward manifestation of inward godliness.

- To be perfect as God commands us to be perfect, requires that we surrender our self reliance and depend on God.

- Our attitudes are expressed through our lives in the form of the Fruit of the Spirit or of the flesh, revealing either godly or ungodly attitudes.

- We conform to Christ's character as we sow the Word of God and pray. The Holy Spirit produces the harvest of godly fruit.

Seek and Apply:

Think about your life for a moment. Are there any areas you have been convinced to change while reading this chapter? Repent, receive forgiveness and Christ's power to change.

Consider the following questions in relationship to your spiritual growth.

1. What has stopped you from pursuing a life of godliness? What can you do to remove that obstacle?

2. Are there any goals in your life that take priority over your goal to attain Christ-likeness?

3. Read Romans 8:28-29. In what context is it that God works all things together for good? How does God use the good, bad and difficult situations of life to shape us into the image of Christ?

    Read 1 Peter 1:6-7; Romans 5:3-4; James 1:2-3.

4. What does God call good in Micah 6:8? Are there situations in your life, presently, in which you could practically apply this Scripture?

5. What are Jesus' instructions for bearing fruit, found in John 15:5-8? What does this mean?

6. How might we guard ourselves from being carried away by erroneous teachings, according to 2 Peter 3:17-18?

7. How can 2 Peter 1:3-8 be viewed when applying the garden teaching to spiritual growth?

8. What important principles in our spiritual growth are seen in the following Scriptures:

    Ephesians 1:18-19

    Jeremiah 29:13-14

    Philippians 3:10-14

9. Concerning our lives, what is the difference between religious ideas of perfection and God's idea of perfection?

10. What are the differences you see between the ladder and garden principles for living life and growing in godliness?

11. Why does God allow us opportunities to face the same challenges several times in our life? How does this differ from the ladder principle? How is it different when it comes to the temptation to get into pride?

12. How are attitudes formed?

13. How is the fruit of the spirit produced in our lives?

Prayer

Father, because You gave Your Son for me, I joyfully give my life to You as a living sacrifice to be transformed into one who lives to honor and obey You. I thank You that by the power of the Holy Spirit who dwells within me I am able to refrain from accepting the world's values and instead put on godly behavior. As I conform to Your pattern of behavior by sowing godly seed into my life, I thank You that I am being changed by the work of the Holy Spirit within, who is renewing and redirecting, changing me in form and function. I thank You that this inward transformation produced by sowing Christ – The Word – into my heart and mind, coupled with the work of the Holy Spirit, is producing multiple harvests of Christ-likeness through my life and glorifying You in it. In Jesus' name, Amen.

For we know that our old self was crucified with him so that the body of sin might be done away with, that we should no longer be slaves to sin—because anyone who has died has been freed from sin.

–Romans 6:6-7

Chapter Three

The Gospel of Jesus Christ: Empowered for Godliness

Jesus proclaims in Matthew chapter five that those who acquire certain attitudes will experience the blessed life of happiness. Before we look into these godly attitudes that characterize Christ, I believe it will be helpful to gain an understanding regarding the revelation shared in chapters five through eight in the Book of Romans. Herein we discover some really good news concerning what we have in Christ and when we receive this news as truth, we are empowered to change in our attitudes and behavior. Please walk with me into the Book of Romans as I share my commentary on these four chapters.

As we transition from chapter four of Romans into chapter five, Paul begins to move from the **how to** of justification to the **results** of that justification, by explaining what we have in Christ. The Book's theme is found in Romans 1:17, *For in the gospel a righteousness from God is revealed, a righteousness that is by faith from first to last, just as it is written: The righteous will live by faith.* It is then expounded upon in the first eleven verses. He begins sharing with the Romans how justification has resulted in peace with God. He explains that peace is available because it is no longer necessary for us to perform our way into salvation. Paul wants his readers to understand that their justification is a done deal and one accomplished by Jesus. It is not by our works, rather, it was achieved by His. This is great news. Christ is our peace, the maker, the matter and the maintainer of it. Therefore, we can enjoy our relationship with God without fear concerning our righteousness. Because we are justified on the basis of faith in Christ alone, we now have peace.

He goes even deeper, explaining that God's grace is not only an eternal salvation, but is a daily salvation. There is a state of grace available to us who live in Christ that gives us 24/7 access to the throne of God. We stand in grace as the gospel takes root in our hearts. This grace grows deep and wide like the roots of an oak tree, anchoring our feet in the Kingdom of God. As we remain under that grace, our character is proven and that proven character results in hope. We rejoice in tribulations, allowing the pressure to transform us into His likeness. Tribulations for Christians produce patience, which nourishes and confirms hope (Romans 5:3-5). We are able to rejoice in our hope, because it is sure. For the unregenerate, this is not so; but for those in Christ by faith, it is. Paul goes on to share that God has poured out His love into our hearts, as He now dwells within us as the Holy Spirit. His power is available to us for every challenge and temptation. As we are convinced of this truth of the gospel, as we accept God's love and allow eternal salvation to become a reality to us, power is released, empowering us to overcome trials and every kind of stronghold. When you know you are saved by grace through faith in Jesus Christ, your hope will not be disappointed.

Paul goes on to explain the love of God. What an amazing thing that while we were enemies with God, He chose us to be His adopted children. He ransomed us, even when we did not know Him, and the debt of our penalty has been paid in Christ. Because we are in Christ we are able to rejoice and glory in God and Who He is. We are able to enjoy all He is and does, because, through Christ, we have received and are able to enjoy reconciliation.

The first eleven verses tell us about the results of justification and what we have through it. Verses 12-23 go on to explain to us "why" we have justification. Paul begins a discussion about sin, the law and Jesus. Sin came into the world through Adam, and along with sin came death to all men. Therefore, the guilt of Adam's sin was upon all men as well. It was imputed to the human race. He explains the nature and purpose of the Law, and how, even before the law was given, men were guilty due to Adam's rebellion. The law was given to show men their guilt and, therefore, need for a Savior. Like an x-ray exposing to a person what is wrong with them, the law shows man what is wrong with him, that without this, he may not be able to see. Although before the law, man didn't know what was wrong or why he was dying, Paul explains that even before the law, before sin was imputed to man, death still reigned.

In Verse 14, Paul calls Adam *a type of the One who is to come* and follows with a contrast of Christ. Thus, we have the first Adam and Jesus is the second Adam, as He came to set right or recover that which had been lost, due to Adam's sin. Paul explained that all of mankind are born "in Adam" and are tainted with His curse and guilt, inheriting death before they are even born. This is the concept of solidarity. We are directly affected by the decisions of those we are connected with. Everyone born is born in Adam's likeness and is affected by His rebellion and curse. Thus the struggle all humans have with sin.

> *God's grace is not only an eternal salvation, but is a daily salvation.*

Christ, as the second Adam, represents many people, as well, but not the same group as Adam. Christ represents all those whom the Father has given Him—those who will accept Him as Lord and Savior. Even though they were sinners, all those, whom Christ purchased, died with Him when He died and rose with Him when He rose. This is an important truth to grasp. Just as Adam's disobedience affected the many he represented, Christ's obedience affects those whom He represents. Humans are born in the likeness of Adam. And those who are in Christ, those He represents, are born again in the likeness of Christ. Also, His righteousness becomes their righteousness. They have been justified by faith in Him. It is not just as if we never sinned, as some try to describe justification. We did sin, and a great price was owed for it. Let's not diminish the gravity of that and the magnitude of God's grace towards us. The penalty has been paid in Christ. We are free, even though we did sin.

Paul made a compelling argument that not only did we sin, but also that the unregenerate man is "under the power of sin and ruled by it"—and that where sin increased, grace increased even more. Some did not understand this gospel of grace, and it resulted in misinterpreting Paul.

Paul had presented this problem in chapter 3 of Romans, but it is in chapter six that he attempts to clarify his message. Many thought the implication of Paul's message in denying the need for works of the law was to encourage sin. The minds of many Jews, including Jewish Christians, held the thought that if the law increased sin (Romans 5:20) and didn't hinder it, then one should increase in sin in order to increase the grace of God. Our fleshly nature tends to lean either towards legalism or lawlessness. Many times we struggle to find the balance. However, Paul begins to show the Roman Christians how it is that the grace of God revealed at the cross not only forgives sins (justifies), but also gives the Christian power over sin (sanctifies). This is an important truth to receive, in order to progress towards our goal of godliness (sanctification).

In verses 1-14, Paul, in presenting the logic of our baptism, details how it is that grace unites us to Christ. He responds to his questions relating to antinomianism by explaining that grace **does not** undermine ethical responsibility and it **does not** promote reckless sinning. He vehemently addresses the false notion that grace gives a license to sin, presenting eight stages of grace. Notice I say stages, not levels. We see stages of growth when sowing seeds, not when climbing ladders.

These stages are:

1. We have died to sin and, therefore, cannot live in what we have died to;
2. We have died to sin through baptism, which united us with Christ in His death. (Because God lives in one eternal moment outside of the existence of time, when we choose Christ, I picture that we are supernaturally placed in Christ to die with Him on the cross.) Thus, my old me died and no longer lives;
3. God wants us not only to share in Christ's death, but also to share in his resurrection life;
4. Our former self was crucified with Christ (a legal death to the penalty of sin) in order that we might be freed from sin's slavery;
5. In the death and resurrection of Jesus: He died to sin once, for all, but He now lives continuously unto God so we should revolt against sin's usurping rule revolting in the name of our new rightful Ruler, Jesus Christ;
6. We are 'dead to sin but alive to God,' just as is Christ, because of our union with Him;
7. We are alive from death and should no longer offer our bodies as tools for sin; instead, we should offer our bodies to God as instruments of righteousness;

8. Because we are no longer under the law, but under grace, sin shall not be our master. "Grace outlaws sin" in our lives and gives us the strength to resist sin's power. All of this explanation is found between the question in the first verse of the first half of chapter six and the last verse, which says grace does not encourage sin. On the contrary, it discourages and outlaws it. In fact, grace gives us the responsibility of holiness.

The second half of chapter six begins again with the same question as to whether grace sanctions sin. Paul presents the same argument, but this time, instead of focusing his emphasis on being united with Christ, he shifts to our enslavement to God. This change is to now emphasize that we have offered ourselves to obey God, whereas Paul's answer in the first part of chapter six emphasized what God did to us—united us with Christ. Paul in verses 15 to 23 is talking of our conversion, our turning from sin towards God. Paul makes the argument that if we have offered ourselves to God as a slave and have committed to obey Him, then we cannot say that we are free to sin.

Paul describes conversion as a transfer of slavery from the master of sin to God as one's new Master; as having believed and obeyed the truth, and as having been set free from the lordship of sin into the Lordship of God. We have, therefore, become slaves to righteousness. Paul uses this analogy because of the Roman Christians' fallen natures and vulnerability to temptation. He is reminding them that they have committed themselves to obedience. He goes even further and draws an analogy encouraging the Christians to now offer, to the members of their body, this process of sanctification, which leads to holiness. Paul goes on to explain a paradox: slavery is freedom and freedom is slavery, saying that once we were free from the control of righteousness, we were then in bondage to sin. Ultimately the benefit was death. But now, being set free from sin, we are slaves to God. Now, instead of experiencing degradation and death, we experience a progressive holiness and the free gift of life.

Paul has made his argument that we need to respond to the devil's arguments, against us and the gospel, by remembering who we are—united with Christ in baptism and inwardly enslaved to God by the self-surrender of conversion. Being united to Christ, we are dead to sin and alive to God. Therefore, we should be committed to obedience and totally obligated to God. As a new life in Christ, it is inconceivable that we would persist in sin.

Paul begins chapter seven of the Book of Romans with a celebration of the readers' release from the Law. He asks them, "Do you not know?" He is referring to their knowledge of the limited jurisdiction of the law, and He asks this question, assuming they do know. He explains that the law only has authority over those who are alive; death annuls it. Therefore, those who have joined in union with Christ in His death are no longer subject to the law, because they have died with Christ. They are, therefore, released from the authority of the law. He uses marriage as an illustration. When a spouse dies, the law no longer applies to the one who is dead, nor to the surviving spouse. The surviving spouse is free to marry another. Those who died in Christ have been freed from the Law. They were also resurrected with Christ and now live as new people who belong to Him. This was the purpose of the death—that the law would no longer apply to them, so they could belong to Christ. Can you see it? This release from the law frees us to serve God in the Spirit and bear the fruit of holiness to God. A discharge from the Law was necessary, in order to receive this new Spirit-controlled life. He concludes that the law was impotent to produce holiness; but in this union with Christ, a life can be produced that glorifies God, due to the strength and power of God working in and through us.

In verses 7-13, Paul gives a defense of the law, explaining that the law doesn't create sin, but it does reveal it. The Law is not our problem. Sin is. Paul defends the law, saying that it didn't cause sin nor does it cause death. Sin is the cause of death. He shows how extremely sinful sin is by showing how it has exploited the Law, which is a holy thing for an evil purpose – death. So the conclusion here is that the Law is good. It is Holy. Law is not our problem, but sin is. Sin has misused the Law.

In the final section of chapter 7, Paul explains that although the Law is Holy, it is weak and cannot produce holiness within us. Paul shows how hopeless the struggle is for those who are trying to live under the law. One cannot hope to walk in godliness in their own strength or just because someone tells them to. The Law shows us what sin is, but it doesn't produce sin. It is our own human natures that produce sin. It is the sin within us that twists the function of the Law from "revealing and condemning" sin to "encouraging and provoking" it. Paul continues concentrating on the law and explains to his readers how sin is like a disease living in us, and the law arouses that sin. Always having been zealous for the law, He basically says he had once felt pretty good about himself until Jesus brought the law to his heart. He depicts himself struggling, trying to please God by keeping rules and laws without the Spirit's help. Self-righteousness had deceived him into thinking he could live a righteous life by himself; but now he realizes it is not only about actions, but about attitudes of the heart. He now wrestles with sin in a whole new way. He speaks of desiring to please God in his mind, yet deep within lies sin, which is opposed to God and opposed to what he wants to do. This vulnerability to sin lies within all of us. When we sin, it is no longer the real us who sins but it is the sin that lies deep within. The old man is dead and we are alive unto Christ as new creatures. The question is, "Do we reckon ourselves dead?" And, "Do we reckon ourselves alive unto Christ?" When we do, we have the power to say "no" to sin.

We need to live in the gospel and allow our union in Christ to be our strength and give us the victory over sin. We need not get into condemnation when we fall, but should repent and allow Christ through the Holy Spirit to help us up. Without union with Christ and relying on that union, sin is stronger. Human willpower is not enough. We need the power of the Holy Spirit, in order to walk in victory over sin. You may ask, "How do we activate that power?" We can activate that power by discontinuing to trust in ourselves and our own strength, and, instead, trust in Christ and His power that lies within us. We have to recognize and choose Christ in us. We have to interpret our life through the gospel. This is an act of faith, just as it was when we quit trusting in ourselves for salvation, but trusted in His work done on the cross. When we did this, conversion took place. When we trust in Christ for our strength to overcome, we find His power.

In Romans Chapter 8, Paul begins with "there is no condemnation" and ends with "there is no separation" for those who belong to Christ. His focus is on the work of the Spirit and the security of the Christian. We find three topical divisions within the chapter as follows: (1) the ministry of the Holy Spirit (2) the future glory of God's children and (3) the steadfastness of God's love toward us.

Paul explains that we are justified by faith, because God condemned our sin in Christ. He took the initiative to do what the law was powerless to do. Therefore, we who are in Christ have the blessing of freedom from any condemnation. Later in the chapter, he explains that no one can condemn us because Christ died, was resurrected and sits at the right hand of God, interceding for us. We have been liberated in Christ from the law of sin and death and no longer look to it for our justification. Paul explains that the law was weakened by our sinful nature, so God made provision through Christ for our justification and sanctification.

Paul makes it clear that we who are in Christ are no longer under the law; now, because of the indwelling Spirit, we are actually able to fulfill the law.

The Law of the Spirit of Life describes the gospel. How the gospel liberates us from the law is explained in verses 3-4.

> Paul makes clear what God did:
>
> - He sent His Son, expressing His sacrificial love towards us.
>
> - He came in the likeness of sinful flesh, simultaneously, as a real human, yet sinless.
>
> - He sent His Son as a sin offering—an atonement for "unwilling sins."
>
> - He condemned sin in the flesh and humanity of His sinless Son.
>
> - He sent His Son and condemned our sin in Him in order to fulfill the righteous requirements of the law in us, who do not live according to the sinful nature but according to the Spirit.

These words *"...live...according to the Spirit"* in 8:4 show us that God's purpose in sending His Son was for more than our justification. It was to produce law-abiding Christian behavior because of the power and presence of the indwelling Spirit. In other words, "although the Law could not secure obedience, the Spirit can, and it should be seen in the Christian life." When God puts His Spirit in our hearts, His law is written there. Holiness is therefore, the purpose of the incarnation and atonement. The moral law is to be fulfilled in us; and, although not necessary for our justification, it should be a fruit of it. Our obedience to the law is so important to God that He sent His only Son to die for us, and His Spirit to live in us, in order to secure our obedience.

Paul develops an antithesis between the Spirit and flesh to explain why obedience to the law can only be possible to those who follow the promptings and surrender to the control of the Spirit, rather than the flesh. Paul explains that our mindset expresses our basic nature as Christians or non-Christians. Our human nature is self-centered, whereas the Spirit's desires bring glory to Christ and form His nature within us. If we are still in the flesh, we are absorbed with thoughts of self-interest, affection and purpose. If we are "in the Spirit" by new birth, then the ambitions and concerns, and what we give ourselves to, are directed by the Spirit.

Our mindset also has eternal consequences, with the mind of the flesh bringing death, and the mind of the Spirit resulting in life and peace. Holiness is the way of life and peace, and those who are in the Spirit set themselves to please God more and more by their submission to the law. Those in the flesh, on the other hand, are unable to please God, because they are unable to submit to His law. Where we set our mind, and how we occupy it, determines our present conduct and our final destiny.

Verse 9 teaches us that the distinguishing mark of the true believer is the indwelling of the Holy Spirit, available to fight and subdue the indwelling sin inherited from Adam. If we do not have Christ's Spirit, then we do not belong to Christ. It is as simple as that. We also see that the Father, Son and Holy Spirit share the same divine essence, and, wherever each is, there is the other also. What power is available to us! We are empowered by the fullness of Almighty God, as we relinquish our battles to Him.

In Verses 10 and 11, Paul proceeds to indicate two major consequences of the indwelling of the Spirit. The first is life, and the second is obligation. Paul tells how, in the midst of our physical mortality, our Spirit is alive. Thus, we have a dying body, yet a living Spirit, because death is a result of sin (Adam's sin), while life is a result of righteousness (Christ's)—the righteous standing He has secured for us. Paul proceeds to explain, however, that the ultimate destiny of the believer's body is not death, but resurrection, because of the indwelling Spirit of life and resurrection. We know that Christ's resurrection is the pledge and pattern for ours. The resurrected body will be a perfect vehicle of our redeemed personality.

Our obligation is no longer to the flesh and its desires, but to the Spirit's desires and dictates. Paul's argument is that we can't simultaneously possess life and court death. He is saying that this is inconceivable. Being who we are in Christ, our behavior should testify to it. We are in debt to the Spirit to live out our life of godliness in Christ and put to death everything that threatens it or is incompatible with it. Paul goes on to say that we are to take the initiative to put to death the misdeeds of the flesh. How? We make a decision and then we carry it out by the Spirit. This is the only way to experience the abundant, satisfied, happy, full life as God's children. We need to follow the leading of the Spirit and continuously remind ourselves of God's awesome love towards us. The obligation we have is mentioned in verse 12.

Here it is again. Our obligation is to live a righteous life! We should live dutiful, upright and blameless before God. And if we are truly His, wouldn't we want to?

The Blessing: Empowerment for godly living:
The Spirit of life secures obedience
in and through us

The Recipient: Those who belong to God
and set their eyes on Him

> *I will give them an undivided heart and put a new spirit in them; I will remove from them their heart of stone and give them a heart of flesh. Then they will follow my decrees and be careful to keep my laws. They will be my people, and I will be their God.*
> –Ezekiel 11:19-20

Reflect and Grow:

Things to Remember:

- The righteous shall live by faith.
- God's grace is not only an eternal salvation, but it is a daily salvation.
- Grace gives us the responsibility of holiness.
- In this union with Christ, a life can be produced that glorifies God, due to the strength and power of God working in and through us.
- Self-righteousness had deceived men into thinking he could live a righteous life by himself; but now as a new creation he realizes it is not only about actions, but about attitudes of the heart.

- We have to interpret our life through the gospel.
- Holiness is the purpose of the incarnation and atonement.
- The moral law is to be fulfilled in us; and, although not necessary for our justification, it should be a fruit of it.
- Our obedience to the law is so important to God that He sent His only Son to die for us, and His Spirit to live in us, in order to secure our obedience.
- The Spirit's desires bring glory to Christ and form His nature within us.
- Holiness is the way of life and peace, and those who are in the Spirit set themselves to please God more and more by their submission to the law.
- Where we set our mind, and how we occupy it, determines our present conduct and our final destiny.
- There are two major consequences of the indwelling of the Spirit. The first is life, and the second is obligation.
- We can't simultaneously possess life and court death.
- We are in debt to the Spirit to live out our life of godliness in Christ and put to death everything that threatens it or is incompatible with it.
- We make a decision and then we carry it out by the Spirit.
- We must be intentional to crucify our flesh. Not just one time, but time and time again, we crucify our flesh over the same thing, to allow the Spirit of God to rule from the throne of our hearts.
- We crucify our flesh by sowing the Word of God and relying on the strength of God.
- Our focus must be on Christ and not on our flesh.
- The unglodly things we choose to allow in our lives are things that we have not yet grown to hate more than we love God.

Consider the following questions in relationship to your spiritual growth.

1. What is biblical justification? On what basis are we justified? What does the behavior look like in someone who understands they have been freely justified?

2. How is it that the grace of God has resulted in our responsibility to holiness? (Romans 6:1-14) How does this make you feel?

3. How is it that we, as Christians, can rejoice in our sufferings? (Romans 5:3-5)

   Do you currently have a situation in your life that you can apply this truth to?

4. What is the concept of solidarity? How does this concept affect us in Adam? In Christ?

5. How does Paul explain freedom as slavery and slavery as freedom? How can you apply this principle to your life?

6. Now, instead of experiencing degradation and death, we experience a _____ _____ and the free gift of _____.

7. How does Paul suggest that we respond to the devil's accusations against us?

8. The law was impotent to produce holiness; but in our _____ with Christ a life can be produced that glorifies God.

9. Living a righteous life is not about actions only. It is also about _____.

10. To evoke the power of Christ to say "no" to sin, we must reckon ourselves _____ and _____ unto Christ.

11. We also must _____ to trust in ourselves and our strength, and _____ in _____ and His power within us.

12. What does Paul explain in Romans 8:3-4 that Christ did for us?

13. How does Romans 8:4 explain God's purpose in sending His Son?

14. What then is the purpose of the incarnation and atonement, according to Romans, as explained in this chapter?

15. What does Romans 8:9 reveal is the distinguishing mark of a true believer?

16. What two major consequences does Paul share, which are due to the indwelling of the Holy Spirit (Romans 8:10-11)?

17. What does Romans 8:12 declare to be our obligation as born-again believers?

18. How do we activate the power of God in our lives?

Prayer

Father, help me to live by the Spirit of Your Word and not knowledge only, living as one who died and has resurrected with Christ to new life. I thank You for Christ, who dwells in me, empowering me for godliness. He is my hope of glory! In His name I pray, Amen.

Do not be conformed to this world (this age), ..., but be transformed (changed) by the [entire] renewal of your mind [by its new ideals and its new attitude], so that you may prove [for yourselves] what is the good and acceptable and perfect will of God, even the thing which is good and acceptable and perfect [in His sight for you].

–Romans 12:2 AMP

Chapter Four

Discovering the Blessing in Godly Attitudes

Now that we have had a commentary on the gospel of Jesus Christ, let us think about our attitudes. We are our attitudes. They are manifested in our daily walk as the fruit of the spirit or flesh. We are known by them. In chapter five of Matthew, Jesus gives us a picture of the attitudes we should be cultivating in our lives. Truly, the Beatitudes are a picture of Christ's character, Himself.

Throughout the next eight chapters we will dig into these attitudes and measure ourselves as to how we are doing in our spiritual life growth. We will not focus on who we are with our un-renewed minds, but on who God calls us to be. In other words, we will take note of where we fall short, take time for genuine repentance, and quickly refocus to the behavior and attitude we see in Christ that is the opposite of what we have seen in ourselves. We do need a realization of the work to be done yet, once we have grieved our sin, we do not want to stay our focus on our shortcomings. We should receive God's forgiveness and move forward leaving that sin and its guilt behind. No one has ever been transformed or had any success in breaking free from sin by meditating on their sin. We are transformed by keeping our thoughts on Christ. This instruction is seen in Colossians 3:1-2 and Romans 12:1-3.

> *Since, then, you have been raised with Christ, set your hearts on things above, where Christ is seated at the right hand of God. Set your minds on things above, not on earthly things.* –Colossians 3:1-2
>
> *So here's what I want you to do, God helping you: Take your everyday, ordinary life—your sleeping, eating, going-to-work, and walking-around life—and place it before God as an offering. Embracing what God does for you is the best thing you can do for him. Don't become so well-adjusted to your culture that you fit into it without even thinking. Instead, fix your attention on God. You'll be changed from the inside out. Readily recognize what he wants from you, and quickly respond to it. Unlike the culture around you, always dragging you down to its level of immaturity, God brings the best out of you, develops well-formed maturity in you.*
>
> *I'm speaking to you out of deep gratitude for all that God has given me, and especially as I have responsibilities in relation to you. Living then, as every one of you does, in pure grace, it's important that you not misinterpret yourselves as people who are bringing this goodness to God. No, God brings it all to you. The only accurate way to understand ourselves is by what God is and by what he does for us, not by what we are and what we do for him.* –Romans 12:1-3 MSG

One obstacle we had before regeneration is that all we had was a list of rules and "do not do's." With an inherent sin nature, we had no power to say no to the sin. As we focused on it, it acted almost like a magnet to the sin nature within us, drawing us to the sin we were told to abstain from. As man concentrated on what he was not to do, his desire to do that thing increased even more. Living in Christ, all things are now lawful, but not all things are profitable, nor are they desired. With our new hearts God has given us, and continues to give us, new desires that line up with His desire for us. Now we have both the example and the power to follow that example, which we have seen and heard in the infinite God-man, Jesus Christ. That is where we want to set our focus. As we focus on Christ, we find ourselves drawing closer to Him, and He drawing closer to us. James declares in James 4:8, *Come near to God and he will come near to you. Wash your hands, you sinners, and purify your hearts, you double-minded.* The Word of God, Jesus, purifies us.

The purpose of this check-up is not condemnation, but realization of where we have been walking and what Jesus desires us to mature into. It is to bring intentionality to our growth. God is so faithful to meet us right where we are and to help us to progress into Christ-likeness. Acknowledge where you fall short, repent where repentance is needed and gain the vision of who you are becoming. This is imperative in removing obstacles to a harvest of godly fruit and Christ-like character.

Matthew 5:3-12 gives us insight to what our attitudes and resulting actions might look like, as we allow our attitudes to be ruled by our reverence for God and by His power and guidance from within. We must be willing to be dead to our selves and our own perceived rights. We lay aside our own desires, thoughts and feelings, and surrender to the Lordship of Christ. We belong to Him, purchased by His precious life. This is our part. We don't have to allow anything sinful in our lives if we don't want it. The truth is, we choose to allow ungodly things in our lives—sins that we have not yet grown to hate "more" than we love God. When our love for God becomes greater than our love for any particular sin, we will "choose" godliness over it. And as we have already seen in the gospel, we are empowered by His Spirit to do so. With the power of almighty God dwelling in us, we have the freedom to follow the Spirit or the flesh. Before Christ freed us from the bondage of sin, we were in a different situation. We were enslaved by sin. That is no longer the case for those who are born again.

To grow in godliness requires a defined goal and an intentional decision made in faith to progress towards that goal, as we allow God control over our lives. What is our motivation to make this decision for this kind of spiritual growth? It is simply a result of our love for God. It is simply because He loved us so incomprehensively to give Himself for us on the cross. It is because we desire fellowship with Him, and without walking in holiness, we are out of touch with His heart and voice. We decide to be intentional about our spiritual growth because God commands us to grow in godliness; and if we love Him, we will set our minds to obey Him.

> *Those who accept my commandments and **obey** them are the ones who **love me**. And because they **love me**, my Father **will love** them. And I **will love** them and reveal myself to each of them.*
> –John 14:21
>
> *Anyone who doesn't **love me** will not **obey me**.*
> –John 14:24
>
> *Make every effort to live in peace with all men and to be holy; **without holiness** no one will see the Lord.*
> –Hebrews 12:14

We must recognize the areas of our lives where God has His finger. Then be intentional to crucify our flesh. Not just one time, but time and time again, we crucify our flesh over the same thing, to allow the Spirit of God to rule from the throne of our hearts. Then we sow the Word of Jesus into our life. Sowing the Word uproots what is not of the Spirit and results in a harvest of Christ's character. Remember, the garden of life will have weeds to deal with. Unwanted plants continually sprout in a garden and must be uprooted and thrown out, in order to prevent their overtaking of the good plants taking root therein. To be maintained, a garden requires diligent work. Perfection (godliness) requires this same kind of attention. It is up to us to sow the seed (the Word of God) into the soil of our lives, water it with prayer, and continually remove any weeds (sins and temptations), keeping the soil of our lives properly prepared to produce an abundance of spiritual fruit.

At the time we received Christ as our Savior, we became a new creation in Christ. Yet some Christians never really seem to experience much change in their lives. I know you do not want that to be you. That is why you are reading this book. But those who have been born again for a number of years and still haven't experienced a changed character, remind me of the caterpillar changed into a butterfly that dies in the chrysalis. The transformation of the caterpillar takes place within the casing. The caterpillar is re-made into a butterfly; but unfortunately, the butterfly can fail to eat its way out of the chrysalis. When this happens, it dies there, never to experience the joy of flying against the background of the blue sky—the life that the butterfly was designed for.

I liken this to the unregenerate person, who, at the time of salvation, is changed into a new, powerful creature in Christ. But in order to enjoy the blessings available to them as a new creation, they must exercise their power in Christ to successfully leave the old life and nature behind. As new creations in Christ, just as the newly reformed butterfly must make an effort to leave the cocoon, we can leave the old life behind as we train ourselves in godliness, in order that we can experience the life we have been created for.

Let's consider our attitudes and see what changes are needed. But first, we should ask, "Attitudes…What are they?" American Heritage Dictionary defines attitude as (a) A state of mind or a feeling; disposition: had a positive attitude about work. (b) An arrogant or hostile state of mind or disposition.[6]

Attitudes are more than fleeting thoughts. They are mental positions embedded into our physical mind. They are a result of our thoughts—in particular, those we have pondered or meditated on. Attitudes form strongholds by forming pathways for the chemical and electrical processes of our thoughts. In other words, attitudes literally change the physical appearance of our physical brain.

Again, note I said thoughts "that we meditate on." We are constantly bombarded with thoughts, without any control over what actually enters our minds. However, we do have the control over what we do with those thoughts. We have the ability to quickly analyze a thought, in order to make a decision as to whether we will reject it or keep it. When we keep thoughts by beginning to meditate on them, they begin to take root in our minds. Soon they become what we call "attitudes" and these attitudes can form good or bad "strongholds." These strongholds become our "default" way of thinking and determine our behavior towards God, ourselves and one another.

Notice I said towards God, ourselves and one another. Many times we think false and untrue thoughts concerning others, and we meditate upon those thoughts. These thoughts then become attitudes. Everything we see that person do is filtered through this ungodly attitude towards them and the stronghold and belief concerning them deepens, even though it is untrue. Soon it is seen in our behavior. If we are not careful, we find ourselves speaking these things to others and helping them to form unjust thoughts as well. It is also seen in our body language when interacting. This is very dangerous and can do a lot of damage to a person as well as to the ministry

God intends for someone's life, especially when our unrighteous attitudes have influenced the attitudes of others towards that person.

> *Likewise the tongue is a small part of the body, but it makes great boasts. Consider what a great forest is set on fire by a small spark. The tongue also is a fire, a world of evil among the parts of the body. It corrupts the whole person, sets the whole course of his life on fire, and is itself set on fire by hell.*
> –James 3:5-6

It is not just the person speaking who is corrupted, but their words spoken against an individual can bring destruction to the entire course of that person's life.

> *Their **tongues** sting like a snake; the venom of a viper drips from their lips.*
> –Psalm 140:3

For those who use their influence with people in an evil way, I believe it will be a serious matter for them on the day they stand before God and give an accounting of their life. Leaders especially must be careful, due to their ability, opportunity and power to influence others either rightly or wrongly. Scripture indicates there may be an accounting for their actions even in this life.

> *O deceptive tongue, what will God do to you? How will he increase your punishment?*
> –Psalm 120:3

> *It would be better to be thrown into the sea with a millstone hung around your neck than to cause **one** of these **little ones** to fall into sin.*
> –Luke 17:2

We need to guard our thoughts, paying close attention to what attitudes are forming in our minds, as our attitudes determine our behavior. And should we have an evil attitude form about someone, other than what we find in

Philippians 4:8, perhaps we need to consider the consequence of our actions toward them, especially should they be a loved and precious child of God (one of these little ones mentioned in Luke 17:2).

This same principle is true for our thoughts concerning God or ourselves for that matter. We need to learn and train ourselves to think the thoughts concerning God and ourselves that God has revealed to us in the Scripture. We can know who God is and we can know who He says we are and accept these Truths by faith. Then we can begin to renew our minds, forming new attitudes that will result in godly behavior. Without knowing God, and accepting His rule in our lives, we will never be satisfied. On the same token, if we do not believe we are who God says we are, we are exhibiting a lack of faith towards God which displeases Him (Hebrews 11:6). In my book, "Experience Real Satisfaction," I have included two full chapters on this topic. At the back of this book, I have included a few Scriptures concerning God's character and the believer's identity in Christ. I would recommend you transfer these Scriptures to 3x5 cards and begin memorizing them.

You may be thinking, "How can I control my thoughts?" To answer that, let's take a look at the nature of a thought. Thoughts enter into our minds in distinct ways. The first way is by the Spirit of the Lord. He speaks to us through His Word, which is alive and is Spirit. He speaks to us through nature and He speaks to us as His Spirit speaks to our spirit, which is now alive in Christ. Our spirit communicates God's thoughts to our mind. When we hear from God, we can know His voice will never be in contradiction to His written Word. Therefore, we should be careful to judge every thought by the Word of God. As we examine thoughts, keep in mind it is not the thought itself that produces sin. It is what we do with the thought that determines our faithfulness. This is where we battle to make the right choice. Thus the common phrase that is used regarding our spiritual formation is that "the battlefield is in the mind." This is where we can and must take control of our lives.

Thoughts often enter through our five senses. Therefore, it is important to protect what we allow into our lives through them. We must guard these gateways to our soul by being particular about what company we keep, what we watch on TV, what we read or view in magazines, what we listen to in music, conversation, etc. Thoughts can also be placed into our minds by the powers of darkness. Have you ever been enjoying your day and suddenly you have an obscene or evil thought come to mind? You wonder, "Where did that come from?" Thoughts may also be deposited through dreams generated by God or by the powers of darkness. Thoughts additionally flow from the area of our physical brain where memories are stored. Here they already live as strongholds. These strongholds are often awakened when we experience a similar incident to one we have lived in the past—one that has been allowed to strengthen through our meditation on it. As the thought or memory from that stronghold is released, or enters our mind in any of the ways discussed here, we have the ability to unconsciously examine the thought and decide whether to keep it or discard it. The stronghold is fortified when we choose to keep and meditate upon the thought, so we only want to keep those that reflect the mind of Christ. We can choose to trash every perception that is contrary to the Word of God, thereby taking the first step to tear down destructive strongholds in our minds. As we replace the destructive reasonings with right thinking, we begin to build godly strongholds in their place. This is our goal, to have God as our only stronghold! Psalm 62:2 NASB, *"He only is my rock and my salvation, My stronghold; I shall not be greatly shaken."*

> *Sowing the Word uproots what is not of the Spirit and results in a harvest of Christ's character.*

I have learned a great deal about the anatomy of a thought and how to change these strongholds in our minds from a book called, *Who Switched Off My Brain?* By Dr. Caroline Leaf.[7] This book has been a great help to me—and many in the Kingdom—imparting insight into the physical nature of our brain and how it relates to the spiritual instructions we find in the Word of God.

Our attitude towards God, life and people needs to be checked often. After all, we are imperfect people living with other imperfect people in an imperfect world. Although as Christians we have been redeemed, the world has not yet been redeemed. People, whether Christian or not, still sin. We, too, carry around with us the propensity to sin, even though we are no longer under the mastery of its power. Sometimes things happen and we question, "Why God, did you let this happen?" It could be a natural disaster or something more personal that brings us grief, discouragement and maybe even bitterness. We may begin to think that God is withholding good from us, as thought Eve in the Garden of Eden. We think He is not answering our prayers, or we think God doesn't love us as much as He does Sister or Brother so and so. I cover many of these questions in "Experience Real Satisfaction" the companion book to this one. There are a number of thoughts common to all, and some that are not so common. In any case, thoughts in direct contradiction to what the Bible says, need to be recognized before becoming strongholds. We discard them by refusing to think upon them. If we have already begun meditating on a thought, it will require more time to remove it. Scripture must be sown to reveal the thought as a lie and allow its power to uproot it. Again, it is normal to have some ungodly or negative thoughts come to mind when life happens, i.e. betrayals, job losses, relationship struggles, financial crisis, sickness, pain and sorrow. But we don't have to keep those that are contrary to the Scripture. We must be diligent at our garden work. Planting the Word of God, watering with prayer and harvesting the fruit of Christ's character is the Christian's work. Just as God commanded Adam to take authority over and guard the garden He had placed him in, He tells us to do the same over the garden of life where He has placed us. He has given us His authority through Christ to rule over it, guarding it from the sin designed to destroy our harvest. If we do not, we find ourselves with thistles and thorns and a life of pain and sorrow, just as did Adam upon his failure to do so.

Thoughts that are opposite from the Word of God will not benefit us, but will harm us. Don't trust your feelings or your circumstances. Trust the Word of God. Situations and emotions are constantly changing and cannot be trusted whereas the Word of God is stable and does not change. Remember that ungodly thoughts open our lives to even more grief. Once we make the decision to reject them, we then choose, by an act of our free will, to think what the Scripture says. Check your thoughts by asking yourself: "Is this thought bringing me life and happiness or does it steal, kill and bring destruction to my life and/or the life of others (John 10:10)? You see, in Proverbs 18:21 MSG, God says, *"Words kill, words give **life**; they're either poison or fruit—you **choose**."* Your words are thoughts before they ever become words. Think about it. Our thoughts, when meditated on, form either destructive or fruitful behavior with corresponding actions.

In Deuteronomy 30:19 God says, *"I set life and death before you, choose life."* I love that. God gives us two pathways, and then tells us which one brings life, as would any good Father. He makes it simple for us. God has told us what thoughts we are to keep, and what attitudes we should have; and He has told us how to walk out our lives so that we may enjoy Him and the life He has given us. 2 Timothy 3:16-17 (NASB), *All Scripture is inspired by God and profitable for teaching, for reproof, for correction, for training in righteousness; so that the man of God may be adequate, equipped for every good work.* God has given us an instruction book that not only leads us to life, but leads us to a life that is full, happy and blessed by God. He has set us apart to be a holy people, who are recipients and extensions of His blessings. We can take control of our thoughts, change our attitudes and begin to walk into the blessed life shared in Matthew 5—a destiny of supreme happiness and great gain. All we need to do is follow His lead.

I want to encourage you to practice applying Philippians 4:8 to your thoughts. In other words, choose to think thoughts that are good and praiseworthy. I choose to think the best about people (most of the time), about myself and about God, rather than the worst. I forget, sometimes, and my husband reminds me, or the Holy Spirit convicts me. I have made a decision to be quick to repent when this happens and get back on track with God. God's instruction to us in this passage is, *"Finally, brothers, whatever is true, whatever is noble, whatever is right, whatever is pure, whatever is lovely, whatever is admirable—if anything is excellent or praiseworthy—think about such things."* That sounds like a command to me. Although I do not do it perfectly, I have committed to it and therefore I am making progress. Making an intentional decision to seek and practice the truth concerning God and the ways of God empowers us to sow seed into our lives that will result in a mature harvest of Christ-like character.

I hope you will join me and commit to a goal of becoming one with Christ which will result in a harvest of Christ on earth.

The Blessing: A harvest of Christ through the blessed one's life benefiting both themselves and others; the personal benefits of peace, joy and satisfaction

The Recipient: Those who, with the help of the Holy Spirit, train themselves with the Word of God to live as one with Christ in what they think, say and do

All Scripture is inspired by God and profitable for teaching, for reproof, for correction, for training in righteousness; so that the man of God may be adequate, equipped for every good work.

– 2 Timothy 3:16-17 NASB

Reflect and Grow:

Things to Remember:

- Thoughts meditated upon determine attitudes.

- Attitudes determine behavior.

- Thoughts in themselves are not a sin. It is what we do with those thoughts that determines whether we sin.

- As we replace the destructive thoughts with right thinking, we begin to build godly strongholds.

- We must be intentional to crucify our flesh. Not just one time, but time and time again.

- To allow the Spirit of God His rightful rule from the throne of our hearts, we crucify our flesh over the same thing multiple times. The flesh is crucified with decisiveness, prayer and sowing the Word of God.

- We choose to allow ungodly things in our lives that we have not yet grown to hate more than we love God.

- We are our attitudes.

- God has given us an instruction book on how we are to think and live.

- We need to train ourselves to think the thoughts concerning God, ourselves and others that God has revealed to us in Scripture.

- Making an intentional decision to seek and practice the truth concerning God and the ways of God empowers us to progress closer to the fulfillment of our goal to sow seed into our lives that will result in a mature harvest of Christ-like character.

Seek and Apply:

Consider the following questions in relationship to your spiritual growth.

1. How do thoughts enter into our minds? When does a thought become a sin?

2. What must we do in order to eliminate sin from our life? How can you apply this to your life?

3. Why is it important to regularly take time to be quiet and consider the kind of thoughts we have been thinking? For your own growth, ask the Holy Spirit to show you what you have been thinking and lead you to the thoughts God desires as the replacement.

4. What is an attitude, and how does it differ from a thought?

5. Have you been relying on your own feelings and emotions to guide you?

6. Can you rely on your feelings as a guide for right thinking? Why? What can you rely on for your guide? Name one Scripture we can use as a foundational guide for testing our thoughts.

7. What other ungodly attitudes are usually present in the environment, where the ladder idea of spiritual development is at work?

8. What is our motivation for entering into, and committing to, a spiritual training program?

9. How is our love for God proven? Does your life exhibit a love for God?

10. What areas in your life is sin ruling? What needs to increase in order for you to choose godliness over that sin?

11. In an environment where the ladder principle is at work, and believers are trying to reach a level where they will never struggle with an attitude issue again, e.g., unforgiveness, patience, humility, etc., what is their underlying goal? How does this resemble what took place when man first fell in the Garden of Eden?

Prayer

Father, I thank You for the written Word. Coupled with the inspired guidance of the Holy Spirit, it is training me in righteousness. I ask that You heal the pathways in my mind and soften the ground of my heart to receive Your Word and develop godly attitudes. Instruct me and empower me to destroy speculations and every lofty thing raised up against the knowledge of God, and to take my thoughts captive to the obedience of Christ (2 Cor 10:5). I thank You for producing godly fruit from the seeds I am sowing and a harvest of Christ into the world. In Your name, Amen.

Hate evil, you who love the LORD, Who preserves the souls of His godly ones; He delivers them from the hand of the wicked.
—Psalm 97:10

Chapter Five

On With the New— Off With the Old

Living a righteous life begins by developing godly attitudes. The attitudes of Christ examined on the following pages should be seen progressively in our lives as followers of Christ. As shared earlier, our attitudes begin as thoughts, and as we meditate upon those thoughts, attitudes are formed. Although our transformation is not attained by striving in our own strength, we are to cooperate with the Holy Spirit in it.

1. It begins, with a vision of Christ and His glory.
2. Next, we get a vision of attaining these Christ-like attitudes. We need to believe we can attain them.
3. We renew our minds to the Word of God and His ways. Spend time in prayer and in the Word, meditating on the Scripture.
4. We have a willingness to allow the Holy Spirit to convict us.
5. We intentionally surrender those areas to Him that the Holy Spirit reveals to us and ask Him to create a godly attitude within our heart.
6. We learn His ways. We intentionally put on the new self while putting off the old.

This putting off the old, by denying its power over us and putting on the new, releases the power of the Holy Spirit in our lives. Spiritual fruit is produced by the Holy Spirit's work in us. We are changed. We put on the new creation by saying to the old, "No, this is not who I am any longer. That was the old me. This is who I am now. I now respond this way and I do this as a new creation in Christ in the authority and power of His name." Speak the Christ-like behavior that you are putting on and begin practicing it in the authority of Christ. The Beatitudes reveal Christ's character to us, and it is His character that we as Christians desire to conform to as His disciples.

Each Beatitude begins with the word "blessed," which is translated from the Greek word "makarios." This word suggests a condition in which congratulations is in order. It is a grace word that denotes the special satisfaction and happiness bestowed upon those who experience salvation.[8] Therefore, the blessedness spoken of in the Bible, a supremely blessed life, is confirmed again to be only available to those who have received Christ as their Savior. This is imperative. As the redeemed of the Lord, we have already agreed that we have an obligation to pursue godliness. I believe this kind of blessedness, as spoken of in the Beatitudes, is only genuinely available to those who are living in the Kingdom of God, not just as a believer headed for heaven, but those living in the Kingdom in a practical sense. Where is this kingdom that we might live in it? It is where God is reigning. It is where Christ is Lord. You can check to see if you are living in the Kingdom of God by asking yourself, "Is Christ reigning as king, or am I sitting on the throne acting as my own Lord over my life?" We choose what areas of our lives to surrender to His Lordship. The goal is to surrender it all—every area. Each Beatitude should be studied with an expectation to change our attitudes and grow in godliness, as we are willing to let go and let Christ reign in these circumstances of our lives. The end result will be fellowship with God and a life of power in the Holy Spirit.

The Amplified Bible translates the word "blessed" as *happy, to be envied, and spiritually prosperous—with life-joy and satisfaction in God's favor and salvation, regardless of the outward conditions.* This is the word Jesus uses, referring to happiness, but this is not happiness as we sometimes think of happiness today. In our modern culture, we tend to think of happiness as a feeling or emotion effected by external circumstances. The happiness Jesus refers to as the blessed life, is not affected by the temporariness of externalities. Again, the Greek word used here also refers to a supremely happy life that is rooted in the depths of the soul and flows from a changed heart where

Christ reigns. It is clear that genuine happiness is a result of a life lived for Christ. There is no other way to discover it. This is the way God created us. He created us for godliness and He created us to be in relationship with Him. Blessedness is not available from the world or any human resource. It is not circumstantial, tangible or emotional. It is divine, deep, lasting and accessible. Blessedness results from a walk rooted in love and the fear of the Lord.

Some of the early movies made about the life of Jesus presented Him as a man who was austere and who rarely smiled, let alone laughed. It is as if the producers of those movies thought seriousness was the definition of godliness. I was so thrilled when the newer versions were made, and we were shown a smiling Jesus. In these newer movies, Jesus is depicted as joyful and happy. I believe this is a more accurate portrayal of our Lord, and what a person looks like that is walking in godliness and the blessedness of God. Jesus indeed had his trials and challenges, yet He had a deep-rooted joy that flowed out of His contentment to be in the Center of Father God's plan and purpose for His life. This is living the blessed life. He was God-centered in all that He thought, said and did. When He grew weary, He spent time with the Father to receive strength and wisdom. He loved and was loved. He had a genuine reverence for God. He declared that He did only what He saw the Father doing. Jesus' prayer was that we (you and I) would be made one with Him as He and the Father were one. *That they all may be one, [just] as You, Father, are in Me and I in You, that they also may be **one in Us**, so that the world may believe and be convinced that You have sent Me* (John 17:21 AMP emphasis mine). Jesus prayed that we would think, say and do as He would think, say and do, as He only does what Father God does. This is oneness. What would Jesus do? How would He think? What would He say? We get a glimpse into the inner attitudes of Christ in the Beatitudes.

The beatitudes also reveal to us the rich blessings available, as we line up our attitudes and lives with God's, becoming one with Him. Remember, these attitudes are not just thoughts, but are strongholds displayed in our lives as a reverence towards God. They are seen in the choices we make. As noted in an earlier chapter, the fruit of the spirit mentioned in Galatians 5:22, 23 (*love, joy, peace, patience, kindness, goodness, faithfulness, gentleness and self-control*) is the outward manifestation of the possession of these godly attitudes. We should ask ourselves what we could do to improve our attitude in each of these areas listed in Matthew Chapter 5. We want to consider how to cultivate these attitudes and take note how doing so results in a blessing for us. As we cultivate godly attitudes, the Holy Spirit goes to work to change us from the inside out, and the evidence of this transformation is seen outwardly in how we live and respond to life's challenges.

I invite you now to join me on a journey to the Mount of Beatitudes in a faraway land called Palestine, where Jesus spoke the most profound, yet simplistic, words ever spoken to a group of people who gathered there. People listened intently as he began with the first word, "happy." May we listen intently as Jesus reveals to us the pathway of godliness, which leads us to genuine happiness and great gain.

The Blessing: Empowerment for godly living: The authority and power in Christ to tear down strongholds and take thoughts captive to the obedience of Christ

The Recipient: Those who walk according to the Spirit

For the weapons of our warfare are not physical [weapons of flesh and blood], but they are mighty before God for the overthrow and destruction of strongholds, [Inasmuch as we] refute arguments and theories and reasonings and every proud and lofty thing that sets itself up against the [true] knowledge of God; and we lead every thought and purpose away captive into the obedience of Christ (the Messiah, the Anointed One).

–2 Corinthians 10:4-5 AMP

Reflect and Grow:

Things to Remember:

- As Christians, we have been given the authority and power of Christ to begin practicing Christ-likeness with an expectation of becoming like Him.

- Happiness is rooted in the depths of the soul and flows from a changed heart where Christ reigns.

- The blessed life in the Beatitudes is experienced by those who live in the Kingdom, allowing Jesus Kingship over their lives.

- These attitudes are not just thoughts, but are strongholds displayed in our lives as a reverence towards God.

- If our goal is to become like Christ, the Beatitudes will challenge the way we think and live.

Seek and Apply:

Consider the following questions in relationship to your spiritual growth.

1. How are attitudes formed?

2. What kind of thoughts have you been thinking on? Do you have some thoughts that need to be taken captive to the obedience of Christ? What areas have you had ungodly thoughts that you meditated on and now have a stronghold in your thinking? Are you willing to uproot that attitude and replace it with it's godly counterpart?

3. How do the attitudes we hold reveal themselves to others?

4. What is the fruit of the spirit (Galatians 5:22-23)?

5. Do you see evidence of godly attitudes in your life? Remember, the evidence is seen in the Fruit of the Spirit.

6. How can oneness with Christ be cultivated? How is it seen in our lives?

7. What does it mean to be *blessed* according to this word's usage in the Beatitudes? What does a blessed life look like?

8. Explain our responsibility and the responsibility of the Holy Spirit in regards to forming our attitudes?

9. Whose responsibility is it to produce the Fruit of the Spirit in our lives?

10. What are the weapons of our warfare alluded to in 2 Corinthians 10:5?

Thank you, Father, that Your divine power has granted to us everything pertaining to life and godliness through the true knowledge of Christ who called us by His own glory and excellence. Thank You for your precious and magnificent promises that by them we may become partakers of the divine nature, having escaped the corruption that is in the world by lust (2 Peter 1:2-4). Thank You for Your presence available to help me surrender to Your Kingship in every area of my life. In Your name, I pray. Amen.

*God blesses those who realize their need for him,
for the Kingdom of Heaven is given to them.*

–Matthew 5:3 NLT

Chapter Six

Happy are the Poor in Spirit

You may be asking, "What is meant by spiritual impoverishment? Let me answer that question, first, by telling you what it is not.

- It is not being without material or financial prosperity or luxuries. However, we do need to be careful not to allow "things" to distract, impede or sever our reliance upon God.

- It does not mean we are to degrade ourselves. Instead, we acknowledge God as the Source of all that we are and all that we have—we praise Him for it.

- It does not mean that we are to be spiritually poor. We are called to grow in our intimacy with God and in holiness. That is the basis of this study.

So what is it to be poor in spirit?

It is not by accident that this is the first beatitude spoken of by Jesus, because without first becoming poor in spirit, one cannot be saved. You see, it is the poor in spirit who recognize they are sinners in need of a Savior.

When we live with the attitude found in Matthew 5:3, it affects every area of life. The poor in spirit recognize where prosperity comes from, and that it is a gift of God. The reality of that recognition is observed in our use of that prosperity, i.e. talents, time and money for God's purposes of advancing His Kingdom on earth and helping others. As we give to God in all of these areas, we are obeying the commandment to love Him with our all.

Those who lack this virtue often have the tendency to exalt themselves by looking down on others. They oftentimes rely on their own goodness and works for righteousness, when, in reality, only God can make anyone righteous. Christ gave us His righteousness as a gift. We need to make a conscious effort to remember that no one begins their walk with God by working for the privilege of righteousness, and no one finishes their walk by earning it. There is NOTHING we can do to earn a relationship with Jesus. There is nothing we can do to deserve His blessing on our lives. Recognizing that anything we attain that has any value whatsoever, or anything we become of significance, is due to the grace of God, enables us to cultivate this character trait that Jesus calls, poor in spirit. It is living in such a way that God alone gets all the glory.

When you live in Christ, and your eyes are on Him and others, instead of yourself and your own needs, you begin to reflect this quality of spirit. God desires that we be focused upward and outward, focused on Christ and others, instead of being self-absorbed. We truly are created to live in this virtue, and we are much happier as we do. As we set our minds on Him, our soul becomes more and more consumed by God. The poor in spirit delight in being totally dependent on God and His grace, and they continually draw their worth, purpose and identity from Jesus.

In other words, they have no exaggerated sense of importance, realizing that in their humanity they are weak. Yet walking in confidence in the power of God, which dwells within them, they believe they can be exceptional and bring fame and glory to His name!

I think this poem by John Oxenham describes the poor in spirit well:

> "Is your place a small place?
> Tend it with care! –
> He set you there.
>
> Is your place a large place?
> Guard it with care! –
> He set you there.

> Whatever your place, it is
> Not yours alone, but His
> Who set you there."[9]

To be poor in spirit is to recognize that all we have is God's gift to us: our very existence, our families, our health, our talents, our situations in life. And even our successes are gifts from Him. For only by the grace of God are we saved. And only by His grace are we able to do anything good at all. It is mind-boggling when we think about the expansiveness of God's grace in our lives. We even pray under the impulse of the Holy Spirit. Romans 8:26-27, *...We do not know what we ought to pray for, but the Spirit himself intercedes for us with groans that words cannot express. And he who searches our hearts knows the mind of the Spirit, because the Spirit intercedes for the saints in accordance with God's will.* And Matthew 10:20, *for it will not be you speaking, but the Spirit of your Father speaking through you.*

Hudson Taylor, explaining his success said, "I think God was looking for a little man, little enough so that He could show Himself strong through him. A man can receive nothing, except it be given him from heaven."[10] Without God, we are nothing and in control of nothing. He truly is our everything! He is our all in all! We need Him in every aspect of our lives, whether we realize it or not.

Look at this promise in Isaiah 57:15, promised to those who develop humility.

> *For thus says the high and exalted One who lives forever, whose name is Holy, 'I dwell on a high and holy place, and also with the contrite and lowly of spirit in order to revive the spirit of the lowly and to revive the heart of the contrite.'* —Isaiah 57:15

God is gloriously enthroned in heaven. Yet, He expands His dwelling to abide also with the "contrite and lowly." God is within you but pride can separate you from experiencing Him. Pride can form a wall within your heart. My friends, I see a lot of unchanged behaviors in the Kingdom of God and a lot of religious veneers. I see a lot of depression and unrest. Could it be due to a lack of humility?

Scripture tells us that the Kingdom of God is righteousness, peace and joy and that the humble are the greatest in it! That means they are the greatest in righteousness, peace and joy! How many of us want those things in our lives? So if we are lacking joy; lacking peace; lacking godly transformation in our life, perhaps we need to consider that, due to pride, we may be blocking God's life from being pumped through our life.

Here is another great promise. *If we Humble ourselves before the Lord and pray, He will heal our land* (2 Chronicles 7:14). He will heal our land—our finances; our friendships; our marriages; our families; our ministries; our bodies; our lives. If we are going to experience the power of God in our lives we must develop an attitude of humility.

So what does a humble heart look like?

Because the poor in spirit and the humble are closely related, we can get a clearer picture of this virtue, as we look at the word "humble." The word humble comes from the root word *humus*, which translates as ground. It is defined as:

1. Marked by meekness or modesty in behavior, attitude, or spirit; not arrogant or prideful.
2. Showing deferential or submissive respect: a *humble apology*.
3. Low in rank, quality, or station; unpretentious or lowly: a *humble cottage*.[11]

You might liken a humble person to the ground composed of clay. God is the Potter and we are the clay. We are in His hands, being formed for His purpose. He can shape us into whatever vessel He desires, and He can reshape us at any time. We need to trust that God is using the circumstances of life to form us. Then we are not dependent on what the circumstances are. We are instead dependent on God. Our trust is not to be in circumstances or anything other than God and His sovereign ways to work His plan through our lives. Although we may hold degrees, positions, abilities, etc., our trust can not be in these things. These items are simply tools that may be used in the hands of God, should He wish to do so. Yet God can also fulfill His purpose without them. The humble knows that it is God's decision as to what He desires to do and how He desires to do it. Therefore, it may be good to have these things, but none of these things in themselves guarantee any level of success or happiness.

I am writing this book in the month of May, four months following the loss of the majority of our congregation. Our friends and those whom my husband had trusted and given opportunity to, men he had spent hours with in prayer and mentoring relationships; and women I had done the same with, all decided to join with another man in the community, who was planting a church. Plans had been in the works for a while, but we were not privy to them. We were taken totally by surprise. He had a lot of money and influence in the community, whereas we had only the Word of God to offer. Their decision meant we lost not only our friends and spiritual family, but we lost the income we had become reliant on. The small group of people who remained were hurt as well because we were forced to move from our building and eventually close. Although we don't like what has happened, we do trust God in it. We asked God, "Are you finished with us here?" And we asked Him to show us His plan for us. We had the power to choose how we would respond in this situation, and what thoughts we would meditate upon. We prayed and by His grace remained faithful to God until He revealed His plan. You see, God is everything to us. More than position, more than people, more than money and the things money can buy. I am not claiming this was an instantaneous response. Especially for me. My husband had to remind me a few times as to the right attitude to adopt in this situation. We chose to remove the weeds (thoughts of rejection and bitterness) that were trying to take root by sowing the Word and thoughts of love and kindness for those who had left. We had to choose to humble ourselves before the hand of God, knowing He alone is sovereign. This wasn't done in our own effort but by relying on the strength of God to help us to do what is right. We believe God can intervene in any circumstance, and, if He does not, then He must have a plan to use it for His purpose. That belief gave us strength and continues to give us strength on our journey.

> *God is the Potter and we are the clay. We are in His hands, being formed for His purpose.*

We know that the old devil had to ask God for permission to sift Job. God allowed it for His purpose. Think of the number of people God has comforted through the retelling of Job's story whether told orally or through the written Word. And how about Joseph who was thrown in a pit by his brothers, then sold into slavery in Egypt. This, too, was for God's purposes. It was God's way to position Joseph in a place where God was able to raise Him to the #2 position in Egypt, where He saved the nation of Israel from extinction. You can read the story in Genesis 37-46. Just as these faithful ones found themselves in situations they did not understand, Christians sometimes find themselves in challenging circumstances that require them to humble themselves before God and admit their helplessness and dependence on Him. We have to cry out to Him for the strength to walk uprightly before Him. Because of who He is, in our weakness, He is strong and gives us His strength. We know that as long as we have God, we have everything we need. In the end God, and His plan, are the only things that matter. Knowing that He promises to be with us and bring us through our battles empowers us to continue.

To truly understand what Humility is, we need to gaze deeply into the nature of Jesus Christ. At the very core of His nature, we will find humility.

> *He who existed as the very form of God, "humbled Himself" and became man, then humbled Himself further by becoming obedient to death for our sake.*
> –Philippians 2:5–8
>
> *Of Himself Jesus said, Learn of me; for I am meek and lowly in heart.* –Matthew 11:29 KJV

When we are poor in spirit, we realize and accept that it is God who decides who will be promoted and who will be demoted. We accept His plan for us knowing that *He works all things together for good for those who love Him and are called according to His purpose* (Romans 8:28). We know that we are being transformed through every situation, the good and the difficult, into the image of Christ to the glory of God (Romans 8:29). We determine to live as a surrendered vessel, allowing Christ to work His purpose and plan through us.

As children of God, we can do everything God calls us to do, because it is the power and wisdom of God that works through us to accomplish His will. When we begin stepping out in faith and seeing the hand of God move through us, we must guard against pride. Oh yea, the temptation is to think "your" prayers are healing the people, "your" message is setting them free, and that "you" saved someone today. In reality, all healing comes from God, who is the Great Physician. It is the Truth—Jesus Christ—the Word, that sets people free. And only God can save a person, as He moves on their heart and reveals Himself to them through the person of the Holy Spirit.

As a student, Jonathan Blanchard, who later would establish both Wheaton and Knox Colleges, prayed this simple prayer: "O my Savior God, deliver me from sluggishness on the one hand and from ambition on the other. May I do all I can do, and feel no more lifted up than if I did nothing."[12]

God is the only One who deserves the glory. To quote my husband, "The truth is this—pride must die in you so God can work through you. It is imperative to remember that it is God who is accomplishing great things for *His* glory"[13] It is not our talent or ability that is succeeding. Therefore, to God goes all the glory in and for all things! He could do it all without us, if He wanted to, but He chooses to allow us to partner with Him. He chooses to work His wonders through us who are housed in these fragile earthen vessels. Working through our weakness, He is glorified as His strength, power and grace become known. I think it is incredible that God has chosen to allow us to share in His work and glory in this way, by moving in and through us. But it is important to remember that it is all Him. We are but the vessels holding and releasing the Power of almighty God!

Once an acquaintance praised Johann Sebastian Bach for his wonderful skill as an organist, and he replied with characteristic humility and wit: "There is nothing very wonderful about it. You have only to hit the right notes at the right moment and the instrument does the rest."[14] There are things that God directs us to do, but He helps us to accomplish those things. And, the results of our obedience are up to Him. He opens doors and He shuts them. He lifts us up and He brings us low. God is in charge, and we owe everything we are and have to Him.

When we have the attitude that reflects poverty of spirit, we recognize and acknowledge our spiritual need and we depend solely on God, rather than on our own goodness. We understand that our own righteousness is as filthy rags. Therefore, we gladly accept the righteousness we receive through the shed blood of Jesus. Again, my husband, quoting William Barclay, put it like this in a sermon he delivered on humility, "Blessed is the man who has realized his own utter helplessness, and who has put his whole trust in God. When a man has realized his own complete inability and has put his confidence in God, there will enter into his life two things, which are opposite sides of the same thing. He will become completely detached from things, for he will know that things do not have it in themselves to bring happiness or security; and he will become completely attached to God, for he will know that God alone can bring him help, and hope, and strength."[15]

In summary, the poor in spirit have a realization that things, positions and awards mean nothing, and that God means everything." It is knowing that we are nothing without Him, but with Him we can be mighty to the glory of His name. The wall of pride is broken down as we put on humility. It is then that we begin to experience the exposure to the other virtues of Christ and begin to act like who we really are—glory carriers of Almighty God.

As we believe we are blessed in our spiritual poverty, we also need to believe the second half of this beatitude. Right now TODAY, we POSSESS the kingdom of heaven. We can enjoy the promise of happiness today! But are we doing so? We need to contend in prayer for the knowledge of the reality and experience of Son-ship, righteousness, comfort, fullness, mercy, peace and great reward. These are ingredients of the Kingdom and they are available to Christians "now" as they cultivate the attitude of "poor in spirit."

The Blessing: Possession of the Kingdom of Heaven Today

The Kingdom of Heaven is joy, righteousness and peace

The Recipient: The poor in spirit, who acknowledge their need for God

Humble yourselves before the Lord, and he will lift you up.
–James 4:10

> **Resulting spiritual fruit:** Love
>
> **Characterization of poor in spirit:** Confident, dependent on God
>
> **Opposite worldly attitude:**
> Self-centered "meism," prideful, yet insecure
>
> **Opposing worldly value:** Personal independence

1. Consider the spiritual fruit produced when you cultivate this attitude. Think of a Scripture that you can sow as seed at times the opposite attitude tries to take root in your heart.

2. Notice the opposite worldly attitude. Compare this to 2 Cor 12:20. Are you being influenced by any of these ungodly vices?

3. Look at the characterization listed above for this beatitude and compare it to its opposing worldly value. How do they differ? Now compare the attitude of one who is poor in spirit with the opposite worldly attitude. What area(s) or circumstance in your life exists that you need to make an intentional decision to lay down the worldly value and/or attitude to pick up the character trait studied in this chapter?

4. To develop this attitude: Consider Psalm 51.

Things to Remember:

- Acknowledge your need for God.

- Cultivate a lifestyle of prayer and surrender.

- Carve daily time out to spend with God, reading the Word even if it is just fifteen minutes per day.

- Spend time in worship.

- Remember to be thankful always.
- Be quick to deflect any glory that comes your way right back to God.
- Become intentional about focusing on God and others and less on self.
- Remember you are nothing without Him.

Seek and Apply:

These questions should reveal to you characteristics of the godly attitude we have discussed in this chapter. As you continue to recognize and depend on God, these character traits will increase more and more in your life.

1. Does your lifestyle reflect your possession of the Kingdom of Heaven? If so, how? If not, why?

2. Reflect on your awareness of your dependence on God. Think of an example in your life where your actions displayed an attitude of one who is poor in spirit. An example when they did not.

3. Think of a time when you turned to God and depended on Him for help? How did that situation turn out?

4. Think about a challenging time when you depended on your own strength, wisdom or money, rather than depending on God. Were you able to fix it yourself? What may have been different had you depended on God, rather than yourself? What kind of anxiety did you experience through the situation?

5. Are you authentic in your relationships? Or do you try to pretend you are someone you are not?

6. What masks are you wearing? Think about why it is you have not been able to remove them?

7. Do you have a joyful countenance, or are you weighed down with the weight of life's responsibilities? If weighed down, could this be a result of trying to do it all and figure it all out without God's help?

8. In what areas of your life do you display confidence in God? In what areas do you struggle?

9. Realizing that things mean nothing and God means everything, give an example of a choice you have made that displays this realization.

10. Review the ways to develop the attitude of humility in your life. If in a group, you may want to discuss these.

Prayer

Father, I declare my utter and total dependence is on You. I thank You to help me to clothe myself in humility towards You and others. I thank You that You have given me worth and dignity and I present myself to You to live for Your purpose on earth. I yield to Your authority and will and resist the temptation to take control of my own life. By Your grace, I resist the temptations of the devil and I choose, instead, to lead a pure life that glorifies You as You empower me to do so. In Jesus' name, Amen.

Blessed Are Those Who Mourn. God blesses those who mourn, for they will be comforted.

–Matthew 5:4 NLT

Chapter Seven

Happy Are Those Who Mourn

Blessed or happy are those who mourn. There are many different kinds of mourning in this life. This Beatitude focuses on one kind of mourning, one in which the Bible equates with repentance.

Had it not been for the fall of man, we would be ruling with God and reflecting the glory of God in our lives. We would have an unhindered, intimate relationship with God. But, because of the sin of Adam and Eve, we have inherited a human nature that is dominated by sin, depraved and desecrating to everything we touch.

As we sin in our walk with God, we not only mourn over the realization that we have been sinning against our Creator and Savior, but we also mourn over the effect that sin has had on our fellowship with Him. This doesn't sound very encouraging to us, but keep reading. Comfort is on its way.

When we acknowledge that every time we sin, we are sinning against God Himself, the seriousness of our sin becomes evident to us. When this increased awareness causes us to mourn over whatever we have done that displeases Him, we experience forgiveness from God, and our contentment is renewed.

Praise God for our Lord and Savior, Jesus Christ! We have great things to celebrate in Christ, and number one on the celebration list is that He has made a way for our forgiveness! But His salvation goes even beyond that. Christ has also set us free from the bondage of sin and, when we are truly mournful of our sin, He restores our intimacy with God. So you see, when Scripture talks about mourning over our sin, God is not suggesting we should walk around with our head hung low and a frown on our faces. God does not desire for us to think about that sin for the rest of our lives.

This reminds me of the account of the Israelites after being held in captivity for 70 years. As they heard Nehemiah read The Law, they began to weep at the realization of their sinful condition and failure to live uprightly before God. Their conviction was strong. But look what Nehemiah then said in Nehemiah 8:10 NIV: *Go and enjoy choice food and sweet drinks, and send some to those who have nothing prepared. This day is sacred to **our Lord**. Do not grieve, for the joy of **the LORD is your strength**.* He went on to encourage them in the mercy of our Lord. God had made a way for their sins to be forgiven through animal sacrifices and was rejoicing that they had turned their hearts back towards Him. When Christians realize the gravity of their sin and repent, they can move forward, praising and celebrating God for His goodness. Our sins are forgiven because of the eternal blood poured out for us by the Eternal One. When we understand the gravity of our sin, though we cannot do anything else but mourn our broken relationship with God, we don't stay in that mournful position. We thank God for the blood of Jesus that restores us! We know He is rejoicing with us, concerning our restoration.

The *Heidelberg Catechism* expresses it:

Q: What is your only comfort in life and in death?

A: That I am not my own but belong to my faithful Savior Jesus Christ.

Q: What must you know to live and die in the joy of this comfort?

A: Three things: first, how great my sin and misery are; second, how I am set free from all my sins and misery; third, how I am to thank God for such deliverance.

Perhaps you wonder how it is that we can experience happiness and satisfaction at the same time we are sad and mourning over our sin? Simply put, it is because happiness and satisfaction are spiritual elements and not circumstantial or emotional. I do want to caution you, however. We should not wipe away the thoughts of our sin too quickly; instead, we should give the conviction of sin a chance to grow into true repentance. Mourning is the outgrowth of true desperation and brokenness for your sin. Think about Job's outlook on his sin: *I despise myself and repent in dust and ashes* (Job 42:6). David, after recognizing his sin in taking another man's wife said, *Against you, you only, have I sinned and done what is evil in your sight, so that you are proved right when you speak and justified when you judge* (Psalm 51:4). Consider Peter in Matthew 26:75 who after denying he knew Jesus *"wept bitterly."* When we mourn over our sin, we will begin to experience true repentance. Repentance is turning away from our sin and facing toward God. The Bible promises that when we repent, God forgives us and cleanses us from the effects of the sin in our lives (I John 1:9). As we experience God's forgiveness, we begin to experience that freedom, satisfaction and happiness, which we have come to expect in our relationship with Jesus (Isaiah 57:15).

Sometimes we are walking in deception and unaware of our sin or perhaps we have avoided admitting to it, even to ourselves. God will then bring it to our attention through another person as He did in King David's story. He used the prophet Nathan to confront him. You can read the story in 2 Samuel 11-12. At other times, He speaks to our conscience through the Scripture or His Spirit to our spirit and mind.

What is it that brings us to this place of genuine mourning? It is beholding our God. When we get a glimpse of the holiness of God, we, like Isaiah, recognize that our goodness is not really good when compared to God. We suddenly have a clearer recognition of our sinfulness. Here is the account of Isaiah, as he looked upon the holiness of God.

> *In the year of King Uzziah's death I saw the Lord sitting on a throne, lofty and exalted, with the train of His robe filling the temple.*
>
> *Seraphim stood above Him, each having six wings: with two he covered his face, and with two he covered his feet, and with two he flew.*
>
> *And one called out to another and said,*
>   *"Holy, Holy, Holy, is the LORD of hosts,*
>   *The whole earth is full of His glory."*

> *And the foundations of the thresholds trembled at the voice of him who called out, while the temple was filling with smoke.*
>
> *Then I said,*
>
> *"Woe is me, for I am ruined!*
> *Because I am a man of unclean lips,*
> *And I live among a people of unclean lips;*
> *For my eyes have seen the King, the LORD of hosts."*
>
> –Isaiah 6:1-5 NASB

But you see, in the very moment we recognize our sin and cry out to God, He removes it from us. We are forgiven. We are cleansed. Look at the rest of the account in Isaiah 6.

> *Then one of the seraphim flew to me with a burning coal in his hand, which he had taken from the altar with tongs.*
>
> *He touched my mouth with it and said, "Behold, this has touched your lips; and your iniquity is taken away and your sin is forgiven."*
>
> *Then I heard the voice of the Lord, saying, "Whom shall I send, and who will go for Us?" Then I said, "Here am I. Send me!"*
>
> –Isaiah 6:6-8 NASB

We clearly see that God doesn't take a lot of time to forgive. When it is done, it is done. *If a man cleanses himself...he will be a vessel for honor, sanctified, useful to the Master, prepared for every good work* (II Timothy 2:21). The Scripture is a New Testament Scripture encouraging us to cleanse ourselves. How do we do that? We cleanse ourselves by calling our sin – sin, then by repenting and receiving God's forgiveness (1 John 1:9). Notice what happened after the angel touched Isaiah's lips and called him cleansed. As our sin is removed, we should be like Isaiah, ready to move forward in the commissioning and purpose of God. This practice of cleansing needs to be embraced in our lives. Again, this is how we keep the garden of life free of guilt, condemnation and insecurity. This is key to keeping our relationship intact with God. We admit our need for the blood of Christ to wash away our sin.

Just as a side note, I want to explain that I don't think all grief comes from letting someone or something take the place of God in our lives. There are other types of mourning although the literal context in the Sermon on the Mount is concerning mourning over our sin. Nonetheless, I believe God has spoken to many through this Scripture for the purpose of comforting them in times of grief, due to the loss of a mate, a child or a parent. Mourning can be the unavoidable and inevitable consequence of loving while we are in this life. It hurt my heart when my mother died on September 30 of 2006. It was my love for her that caused me to grieve her absence. Yet God does not want us to withdraw our love from people, in spite of the fact that loving can inevitably bring pain. He doesn't promise to take away the pain, but He does promise to comfort us in it. And His comfort is not like the sympathy we get from people, but rather the very nature of the Holy Spirit Himself Who calls Himself the Comforter. Another example of grieving in my life was when my husband abandoned me for another woman. In both of these instances, the Holy Spirit strengthened me and brought me once again to a life filled with joy. Jeremiah 29:11 is a great verse to hold onto during times of loss. *For I know the plans I have for you,* declares the LORD, *plans to prosper you and not to harm you, plans to give you hope and a future.*

If you find yourself in a time of grieving the loss of a loved one, whether through death, sickness, divorce or abandonment, please know that the Holy Spirit is with you and He will hold your hand through the various stages of grieving your loss. It is a process and it takes time to heal our losses. I especially believe death is so difficult for us because we were created as eternal beings, to live forever. Our emotions were not created to handle death. Death is a result of the fall of man, when he sinned against God. But through the death and resurrection of Christ, God has sent the Holy Spirit to comfort us. We can know that He will be faithful to bring us through to the place where we will be able to enjoy the good memories, without the pain of the absence. Meanwhile, we can hold on to the promise we have in Him of eternal life. It helped me when grieving the death of my mother to remember that I will see her again! *Weeping may last for the night, but a shout of joy comes in the morning* (Psalm 30:5b).

> *Happiness and satisfaction are spiritual elements.*

The Blessing: God's forgiveness:
All obstacles to relationship with God are removed; the effects of sin are removed resulting in comfort and restoration of contentment and satisfaction

The Recipient: The one who acknowledges their sin as sin and is sorrowful for it

I tell you the truth, you will weep and mourn while the world rejoices. You will grieve, but your grief will turn to joy.
–John 16:20

Reflect and Grow:

Resulting spiritual fruit: Joy

Characterization of those who mourn: Open to receive conviction and quick to repent due to realization of the gravity of their sin against God

Opposite worldly attitude: Decadence, no sense of responsibility

Opposing worldly value: Happiness based on externalities; immediate gratification at any cost, the detriment of others or even at the cost of an intimate relationship with God

1. Consider the spiritual fruit produced when you cultivate this attitude. Think of a Scripture that you can sow as seed at times the opposite attitude tries to take root in your heart.

2. Notice the opposite worldly attitude. Compare this to 2 Cor 12:20. Are you being influenced by any of these ungodly vices?

3. Look at the characterization listed above for this beatitude and compare it to the opposing worldly value. How do they differ? Now compare the attitude of mourning with the opposite worldly attitude. What area(s) or circumstance in your life exists that you need to make an intentional decision to lay down the worldly value and/or attitude to pick up the character trait studied in this chapter?

4. To develop this attitude: Consider James 4:7-10.

Things to Remember:

- Be diligent to maintain an open attitude to receive conviction about sin.

- When God reveals sin in your life, be quick to repent (accept responsibility for and confession of sin) and receive forgiveness (1 John 1:9).

Seek and Apply:

Attitude Check-up: Think about your life for a moment.

1. When you confess your sin, do you do it casually and expect God to forgive you and cleanse you? Or do you think about the GRAVITY of your sin and allow the conviction to bring you to a place of TRUE REPENTANCE? Think for a moment about the difference. If in a group, discuss the difference between a casual versus a true repentance.

2. Once you are truly repentant, do you leave the past and move forward with God? If not, what is holding you back? How would holding onto your guilt affect your relationship with God? How might it affect your behavior?

3. What does the Christian who mourns over their sin experience?

4. How does God comfort the Christian who mourns their sin?

5. Examine your life now and ask God to reveal to you any areas of uncleanness.

It may help to play soft instrumental music. As you do this, remember everything is received in the Christian faith by faith and not by sight. The same holds true with receiving God's forgiveness. It is not a feeling—it is a gift from God received in exchange for acknowledging sin and mourning over the resulting broken fellowship with God. There is only one thing worse than sin, and that is to deny it.

In order to hear God's voice, pray for the Holy Spirit to quiet your soul. Then take time to repent of those sins. Receive His forgiveness and cleansing.

To help you get started: Ask God to show you any sins as you think about your relationships. Think about your work. Think about your actions towards others. Have you stolen? Committed adultery? Cheated? Sexual sins? Do you have anything or any one on the throne of your heart where God belongs?

Take time and truly repent. Then receive by faith the promise of 1 John 1:9, *"He cleanses us from all unrighteousness,"* and live as a blessed and highly favored child of the living God. Choose to believe God. If you have repented, you are forgiven.

Prayer

Father, search me for any sin I have committed against You. Reveal such to me and give me genuine sorrow for it. Do not cast me away from Your presence but help me to be quick to receive Your forgiveness and restoration as I am quick to repent. I pray as did David in Psalm 51:6-11a, Behold You desire truth in the inward parts, and in the hidden part You will make me to know wisdom. Purge me with hyssop, and I shall be clean; Wash me, and I shall be whiter than snow. Make me hear joy and gladness, That the bones You have broken may rejoice. Hide Your face from my sins, And blot out all my iniquities. Create in me a clean heart, O God, And renew a steadfast spirit within me. In Jesus' name, Amen.

God blesses those who are gentle and lowly, for the whole earth will belong to them.

–Matthew 5:5 NLT

Chapter Eight

Meekness Leads to Rest

In verse 5 of Matthew 5, God tells us that the one who is *Blessed (happy, blithesome, joyous, spiritually prosperous—with life-joy and satisfaction in God's favor and salvation, regardless of their outward conditions) are the meek (the mild, patient, long-suffering), for they shall inherit the earth!* (AMP) These blessed people are those whom we call meek and patient. What kind of inward qualities does a meek person have that brings such supernatural peace to their inner being?

For one thing, they are content with God about the way He made them and the life He has given them. <u>The Message Bible</u> puts it like this, *You're blessed when you're content with just who you are—no more, no less. That's the moment you find yourselves proud owners of everything that can't be bought.* This kind of peace cannot be purchased with any amount of silver or gold.

The meek man cares not at all who is greater than he, for he has long ago decided that the esteem of the world is not worth the effort. After all, the world's esteem is fleeting. Should you have the world's esteem, you know how difficult it is to keep it. I send a word of caution to the one who has it.

One day you will surely fall off that pedestal, if not from a change in how people view you, from pure exhaustion of trying to be who they expect you to be. Therefore, learn to be who God has created you to be and quit worrying over what others think you should be.

I do think God desires us to walk in transparency and quit pretending in order to please others. God's opinion is the one that counts. I am not talking about purposely acting in ways that offend others. We should always consider others before ourselves and how our actions may affect them. However, we have to realize that when it comes to pleasing people, the old saying, "You can't please all the people all the time" really does have merit. You will experience much more rest in your life if you love God, keep His commandments and just be who God made you to be.

God has given each of us a unique personality and spiritual gifts, according to His own wisdom. Realizing and accepting this truth makes it much easier to love people as God created them. Those who are in Christ are His workmanship. I don't need to be like them and I don't expect them to be just like me. We are indeed at rest when we accept God's hand in designing our lives. How exhausting it is to pretend. If you have felt the need to pretend in order to glean the acceptance of those you care about, it will take some courage at first to remove the mask. I promise you, the needed grace will follow, as you learn to share in this new and easy yoke with the Christ. Jesus encourages us, *Take my yoke upon you and learn from me, for I am gentle and humble in heart, and you will find rest for your souls, For my yoke is easy and my burden is light* (Matthew 11:29-30).

When temptation strengthens and you find yourself about to put the mask on again, remember this… The value of an item is determined by what is paid for it. If you have received Christ as your Savior and Lord, then the ultimate price has been paid for you. God has determined your value to be the life of God Himself. Can you see how valuable you are? The Creator deemed you to be worth the price of His only begotten Son. God's opinion of you will encourage you and result in peace, whereas the praise of people will always disappoint you. The world's opinion is fickle and unreliable. Only a very foolish person will put their trust there. Besides, as you and I both know, no one in the world has a worth valued higher than the Son of God; so do not allow someone's opinion to carry more weight than His. Receive your esteem from Christ.

Sometimes meekness is equated with being mealy-mouthed, but that is not a correct picture of meekness. Meekness does not connote weakness, but rather "controlled strength." I have heard several Christian teachers and preachers use "meekness" to describe a wild stallion that has been tamed and bridled to the point that he now yields to being ridden. That stallion still has all the strength it had when it was wild, but his strength is now under control. The stallion has surrendered his strength to his master's direction. We are not talking about "cookie-cutter" Christians as some may think. Meek men and women still have their personality and strengths, but they have surrendered all their life to be directed by the Spirit of Christ.

Meekness and humility are interwoven throughout Scripture. We see examples of these character traits in the lives of the Apostle Paul, Jesus and King David. Paul's meekness is seen in the way he assesses himself in regarding others more highly than himself. Note the progression of his growth in meekness in his choice of comparison. In 1 Corinthians 15:9, he states that he is the least of all apostles – *For I am the least of the apostles and do not even deserve to be called an apostle, because I persecuted the church of God.* Then he says in Ephesians 3:8 that he is the least of all the saints – *Although I am less than the least of all God's people, this grace was given me: to preach to the Gentiles the unsearchable riches of Christ.* His last assessment was that he is the chief of sinners in 1 Timothy 1:15 – *Here is a trustworthy saying that deserves full acceptance: Christ Jesus came into the world to save sinners—of whom I am the worst.*

> *The meek man cares not at all who is greater than he, for he has long ago decided that the esteem of the world is not worth the effort.*

Jesus, of course, is the greatest example of all. The essence of humility and meekness are exhibited through His willingness to leave heaven and come to earth as a man. He does not exalt Himself as God and deliver Himself from the plan and purpose of God, but willingly submits to the cross, in order that you and I could be saved and reconciled to God. No man will ever exhibit such love for others, putting others before themselves and laying their life down that others might live, to the degree that Christ Jesus has done. It is beyond comprehension that God Himself would exhibit such meekness to come to earth as a man for us, even though we were at enmity with Him. The example of His humility and meekness is summed up in Philippians 2:1-8a:

> *"If you have any encouragement from being united with Christ, if any comfort from his love, if any fellowship with the Spirit, if any tenderness and compassion, then make my joy complete by being like-minded, having the same love, being one in spirit and purpose. Do nothing out of selfish ambition or vain conceit, but in humility consider others better than yourselves. Each of you should look not only to your own interests, but also to the interests of others. Your attitude should be the same as that of Christ Jesus: Who, being in very nature God, did not consider equality with God something to be grasped, but made himself nothing, taking the very nature of a servant, being made in human likeness. And being found in appearance as a man, he humbled himself and became obedient to death—even death on a cross!"*

Power and strength under control, the willingness to submit to God's will, and the willingness to put others before oneself, are seen in Christ. These are all characteristics of one who is meek.

Before Christ, we see Abraham, while he was still called Abram, exhibiting the quality of meekness in Genesis 13. Lot, Abram's nephew was traveling with Abram, and both had a great number of possessions in flocks, herds and tents—so great that the land could not support them. Quarrels arose between Lot's herdsmen and Abram's herdsmen. Abram, desiring to keep peace between himself and Lot, suggested that there was plenty of land for the two to choose from, so why not part company. We see Abram's meekness displayed, as he allows Lot to choose the best land, the Jordan Valley, where the land was well watered and green. Abram gave up his right to choose first and took the land that appeared second best. Are you beginning to understand the character quality of meekness?

Let us look at another example of meekness. We see Moses being challenged in Numbers 11-12. The people began complaining about their hardships and expecting Moses to do something about it. Then the riffraff (as The Message Bible calls them) among the people began craving meat and soon had the people of Israel complaining. Moses heard the whining of the people continuously.

Next Moses' brother Aaron and his sister Miriam began talking about Moses behind his back. They questioned his decision to marry a Cushite woman, and they questioned his spiritual leadership saying, *Is it only through Moses that God speaks? Doesn't he also speak through us?* (Numbers 12:4 The Message Bible). God heard this, and called the three of them together; their attitudes were revealed to Moses', and God's judgment fell on Miriam in the form of leprosy. Through all of this, Moses remained meek. He did not become defensive. *Aaron said to Moses, 'Please, my master, please don't come down so hard on us for this foolish and thoughtless sin. Please don't make her like a stillborn baby coming out of its mother's womb with half its body decomposed.' And Moses prayed to GOD: Please, God, heal her, please heal her* (The Message Bible).

Moses could have retaliated and spoke curses on Miriam for her attitude and actions against him. Yet he displayed self-control, and he chose the godly response in the situation. A meek person does not see themselves as a victim, but as one in control of their choices and responses. They choose how they will respond to the hurt done against them. The best definition of meekness I have found in the Bible is Proverbs 16:32, . . . *It is better to win control over yourself than over whole cities* – TEV. Jesus could have retaliated and called twelve legions of angels to His rescue. But He was on a mission. He chose to fulfill His purpose for coming to earth, and He forgave those who persecuted him.

Then there are the "3:16" verses, where meekness and humility are so clearly demonstrated:

> John 3:16, *For God so loved the world that he gave his one and only Son, that whoever believes in him shall not perish but have eternal life.*

> 1 John 3:16, *This is how we know what love is: Jesus Christ laid down his life for us. And we ought to lay down our lives for our brothers.*

> Colossians 3:16, *Let the word of Christ dwell in you richly as you teach and admonish one another with all wisdom, and as you sing psalms, hymns and spiritual songs with gratitude in your hearts to God.*

In reality, meekness is an attitude of humility and submission to God. Those who are meek continually look to God to give them life and blessings and the Scripture says *they will therefore inherit the land*. This is in contrast to those who live separated from God and attempt to take possession of the land and wealth by evil means, instead of looking to and trusting in God. When I say by evil mean, you may be surprised to know that any means that does not include God is evil. Matthew 6:33 tells us that we are to seek the Kingdom of God first and then all the other things we need and even some of those things we desire will be given to us. Timothy tells us that God gives us all things for our enjoyment. The key to enjoying the things in our lives is not to seek after them ourselves. Instead, seek God and let Him give these things to us.

There is a place of rest that God has for those who are meek, a place where all striving ceases and a child of God surrenders to the will and purpose of God. A man or woman who has learned meekness can follow, they can go last, they can be transparent, and they can recall their vulnerabilities without feeling threatened or defensive. A meek person regards others more highly than themselves, renounces their rights instead of fighting for them, and is not easily offended. This is freedom, my friend. And you can have this kind of freedom. You can choose your reactions to any given situation, because of the Spirit of Christ Who dwells in you. How will you choose to react to those people who hurt you in your future? Because the question is not "will people hurt you," because they inevitably will. And no one in life avoids hurt. But we do have the power as well as the ability to respond in meekness and receive God's blessing and transformation.

God has given each of us a unique personality and spiritual gifts, according to His own wisdom.

I recall a time several years ago, when I had shared a ministry idea with a friend. Two months later, she declared to the world that God had dropped this wonderful idea into her mind. There was no mention of me, or what I had shared with her. Although there were a few minor differences, the vision was the same. Now I had a choice to make. I could be upset and angry, or I could just move forward. I decided it was not worth suffering in my relationship with God. I chose how I would think about the situation. I said to myself, "perhaps God has given the idea to me knowing I would share it with my friend. Perhaps His plan all along was then to expand on it and launch it through her leadership." After all, she had more contacts and influence than I and could probably take it much further. I thought He was going to be able to do so much more with it through her, than through me. I just praised Him for using me to ignite a spark in her.

Don't get me wrong. God had to work with me on this. I didn't get to this point overnight. At first I struggled with thoughts of, "How dare she? That's my idea, and, why doesn't she at least give me some credit for the conversation we had?" But I chose not to meditate on those thoughts. Knowing I am the captain of my own thoughts, I chose to take my thoughts captive to the obedience of Christ. I praised God for advancing the Kingdom through her. After all, that is what really matters, isn't it?

To expound on this story further, she offered me the opportunity to minister with her, and I did for a short time, but it became evident that she was struggling with my involvement. Perhaps she had guilt feelings. I really do not know. I cannot read the minds of others, nor do I know what is in their hearts. All I know is I wanted to put her needs above my own and walk in meekness in this situation. I knew what was required, and I made the decision. As much as I wanted to be involved with this group, I told her I was removing myself from the ministry. I felt my involvement was bringing unnecessary stress upon her and I told her my friendship with her meant more to me than to allow this to come between us. I truly was cheering for the success of the ministry. I hoped to save the friendship, but, unfortunately, I failed. Her response to my decision was not what I had hoped. But God knew my heart was to respond in meekness, and He gave me the rest I needed to make this decision. Situations like these give us opportunities to choose our thoughts and responses. Why choose ungodly ones when we can maintain our intimacy with God by choosing to put others before ourselves? We have His power to do so. And think about this… Our rewards in heaven are eternal, whereas here they are so very temporal.

About a year later, I had a similar thing happen again with someone else. This time it was almost second nature for me to just let it go. I reached for God, sowed the Seed and it was done. How exciting it is to have the opportunity to see that God has indeed changed us. I still sowed the seed of Christ but there was very little unrest involved, unlike before. This time, the friend responded favorably and appreciated my heart and willingness to allow her to move forward with this opportunity while loving her. I believe this moment was the beginning of a huge inward character change for her. What a wonderful opportunity to be a reflection of Christ to others and allow the power of His glory to change them. What a wonderful rest we have, as we accept that God is in control.

I love this quote from A.W. Tozer in *The Pursuit of God*. It speaks to a common misunderstanding concerning meekness: "The meek man is not a human mouse afflicted with a sense of his own inferiority. Rather, he may be in his moral life as bold as a lion and as strong as Samson; but he has stopped being fooled about himself. He has accepted God's estimate of his own life. He knows he is as weak and helpless as God has declared him to be, but paradoxically, he knows at the same time that he is, in the sight of God, more important than angels...He knows well that the world will never see him as God sees him, and he has stopped caring."[16]

Mr. Tozer understood that godly meekness is not the same thing as feelings of inferiority. True meekness does not come from a lack of confidence or a lack of boldness. It comes from finding adequacy and fulfillment in God alone.

Jesus says, when we begin to walk in meekness, displaying control over our reactions to life, circumstances and relationships, we will be blessed. Perhaps you are thinking, "That leaves me out! I can't control my reactions! I get so mad, so hurt and I just can't help what I feel!" You are right. You cannot do this on your own. You have to surrender these feelings to Jesus and let God's healing spirit empower you as He fills you moment-by-moment. We don't live the Christian life on our own, nor can we by ourselves change ourselves. We change by allowing Christ to live in us, so that He can shape us into whom He has called us to be. He will break those negative patterns of defensiveness and replace them with godly attitudes of love and self-control (2 Timothy 1:7) as we surrender to Him, follow His guidance and receive His strength. A.W. Tozer described meekness this way: *Jesus calls us to His rest, and meekness is His method.*[17]

In a nutshell, if we want to walk with an attitude of meekness, we must surrender our situations to God and allow the Spirit of God to direct our steps. Whatever part He has for us to play in His story on earth, is right and the best plan for us—whether standing on a platform preaching to hundreds or thousands or pasturing a church of 50...serving behind the scenes or serving by lifting the arms of our leader. Whether teaching the children or cleaning up after them. Whether a homemaker or a professional working outside of the home. One thing is as important as the other, if it is God's assignment to us. It is humbling just to be a part of what God is doing on the earth.

The Blessing:
Live in peace; Inherit the land; Experience God's favor in life

The Recipient:
Those who quit striving with God and others; They have surrendered their life to God and find adequacy and fulfillment in Him alone

The lowly will possess the land and will live in peace and prosperity.
–PS 37:11 NLT

Reflect and Grow:

Resulting spiritual fruit: Peace

Characterization of the meek: Humility, submission, self discipline

The opposite worldly attitude: Self-exaltation; lust for control and position

Opposing worldly value: Power

1. Consider the spiritual fruit produced when you cultivate this attitude. Think of a Scripture that you can sow as seed at times the opposite attitude tries to take root in your heart.

2. Notice the opposite worldly attitude. Compare this to Galatians 5:19-21. Are you being influenced by any of these ungodly vices?

3. Look at the characterization listed above for this beatitude and compare it to its opposing worldly value. How do they differ? Compare meekness with the opposite worldly attitude. What area(s) or circumstance in your life exists that you need to make an

intentional decision to lay down the worldly value and/or attitude to pick up the character trait of this beatitude?

4. To develop this attitude: Consider Matthew 11:27-30.

Things to Remember:

- Stay surrendered to Christ, knowing He is in control of the affairs of your life.
- When others take, give.
- When others hate, love.
- When others abuse, reach out and serve them.
- Live your life as though you have no rights, caring for others' needs before your own.
- Stay close to Christ. Give your burdens to Him and allow Him to carry the load.
- Spend time with God and ask Him to fulfill you with His love.
- Find contentment in the knowledge that God is in control and knows what is best for you.
- Develop a disciplined and godly response to life, circumstances and relationships.

Seek and Apply:

Attitude Check-up: To examine your life for meekness, ask yourself:

1. Do you find yourself wishing you had someone else's life? Their giftings? Position? Job? House? Family? Material things? Are you content with whom you are, no more and no less?

2. Are you quick to listen and slow to speak (James 1:19), putting a guard over your mouth? Think of a time you were not? Think of a

time you were? It is out of the heart that the mouth speaks (Matthew 12:34) and your words will testify to your meekness or lack of it. How have you seen this statement to be true in your own life and the life of others you know?

3. In what ways are you operating as a bond servant, loving Christ as your Master and serving in His household, the church? If you are truly operating as a bond servant, then you will have no problem with being treated like a servant. Do you find yourself getting offended at times, feeling as though you are being treated this way?

4. How do you respond when others are successful and receive affirmation, even when you do not? How do you feel?

5. How do you respond when you are not chosen, or you are last? Do you always have to be first? Meekness is exhibited when we can be happy to let someone else receive the prize.

6. How do you react in hurtful situations? Defensively, with anger and malice? What steps can you take when someone does something that causes you pain?

7. Think of an example of when you responded in meekness to a hurtful situation.

8. In what kind of situations are your feelings controlling you? What can you do to take this control back?

9. In what kind of life situations do you find it difficult to exhibit meekness? Now that you are aware of these, ask for God's help to change. Be intentional about recognizing the opportunities to display meekness with the help of the Holy Spirit working in you.

10. Meditate on Psalm 17:14, "O Lord, by your hand save me from men of this world whose reward is in this life." What is God speaking to you? Now turn this Scripture into a prayer.

Prayer

Father, help me to humbly accept the life You have given me. I will to surrender my life to You for Your purpose. Help me to know You more and to grow in meekness that others may see You through my life. I release to You my burdens of sin, weariness, oppression & persecution and of excessive demands from myself and others, and I take up Christ's easy yoke of communion. I thank You that as I walk out my life in intimacy with You, You change what was meaningless, wearisome toil into spiritual productivity and purpose. In Your name I pray, Amen.

Blessed are those who hunger and thirst for righteousness, for they will be filled.

–Matthew 5:6 NIV

Chapter Nine

Hunger and Thirst for Right Standing with God— and Be Satisfied

The Amplified Bible composes the above verse as, *Blessed and fortunate and happy and spiritually prosperous (in that state in which the born-again child of God enjoys His favor and salvation) are those who hunger and thirst for righteousness (uprightness and right standing with God), for they shall be completely satisfied.*

I love this—"completely satisfied." Righteousness is a "legal term" in the Kingdom of God. This verse tells us that, legally, we have right standing with God, because Christ exchanged places with us. Jesus took our deserved place on the cross and gave us His righteousness for which we did nothing to merit. We are now clothed in the righteousness of Christ Jesus. His righteousness was perfect righteousness, because He led a perfect life, then was obedient to God and paid the penalty for our sin.

Righteousness is also a "relational term" in the Bible in that it describes the relationship between a born-again Christian and God. Being in a state of righteousness is being right in your relationship with God and others, and living your life in a way that agrees with God. I recall a time in my life that I loved God but I was not living uprightly before Him.

Feelings of rejection poisoned my early life after an abusive marriage. I felt as though I was a failure as a woman. I desperately tried to prove to myself that I was attractive and desirable. I was desperate to experience true love, and I was looking for it in all the wrong places. Some nights I would have multiple dates lined up, in an attempt to discover it. Yet I felt so lonely and so unloved. Then a working associate began to talk to me about Jesus. I turned my focus towards God and asked Him to change my heart and direct my steps. My relationship with Him became the focus of my life. Changes in my life were almost instantaneous, as I began to experience His love and acceptance. My thirst for righteousness could not be quenched, and God's presence began to fill my very soul. I continue on that same path today, hungering and thirsting for God and the ways of God. Satisfied with His love and the knowledge that I am growing daily in deeper relationship with Him. I want His life to flourish through my life. I know my debt has been paid, and I know Jesus clothed me in a righteousness I could never have earned. But I also know that my God desires that I live a godly life before Him. And because I love Him so much because of what He did for me, I can do nothing less than to train myself in His ways and with His help, set a goal to grow and mature into His image.

Genuine happiness does not come from things that can be acquired in the world. It is only found in Christ and in living a godly life. Although we do have physical needs that must be met, true soul satisfaction does not come from simply having our physical needs met. True soul satisfaction comes when our hunger for spiritual things—the things of God—are fulfilled. Matthew 6:33 tells us to seek first the kingdom of God and His righteousness and then all those other things—the natural, physical needs we all have—will be added to us. In other words, when we take care of God's business, then He will take care of ours. It is not that the pursuit of other things is wrong in itself. Our pursuit is wrong when it doesn't flow out from the primary pursuit of God. It is wrong when it isn't a result of our first pursuing God.

> *Being in a state of righteousness is being right in your relationship with God and others, and living your life in a way that agrees with God.*

If you don't know where you are going, you will wind up somewhere else. So, set your mind on the things of God, first and foremost. Paul charged the Christians in Colossians 3:2 to *"set your mind on things above."* Then he challenged them to *"put on"* godly virtues, by which he meant to live *godly lives.* Hungering for righteousness is desiring to have life God's way! It is seeking God's uprightness and justice rather than having confidence in oneself and one's own ideas of what is good. We cannot look to ourselves, or others, to find what is good. We must look at God. He alone is good and sets the standard for us. His Word is our measurement and what we must compare our walk to.

Do you remember the movie, Attack of the Clones? Anakin Skywalker becomes attached to things and becomes the evil Darth Vader. In his journey to the dark side, he is unable to surrender his mother and his girlfriend to God, or to trust and accept His plan for their lives. His unhealthy attachment results in an obsessive desire to act as his wife's protector and god. Becoming attached to things or people in an ungodly way opens the door to darkness. When we try to be our own god and provide for ourselves instead of trusting God to do it, we will soon find ourselves enslaved again to the one Christ has set us free from. This fear is rooted in an unwillingness to accept God's sovereign rule over our lives. Seeking more of God, to understand His ways and to know His character, will help relieve your fears. Prayer and maintaining a heart of praise and thanksgiving will also help alleviate your anxiety. Philippians 4:6 encourages, *Do not be anxious about anything, but in everything, by **prayer** and petition, **with thanksgiving**, present your requests to God.* Bottom line, is we must keep our focus on Christ and living uprightly for Him. We then trust that He will take care of everything else. Hebrews 11:6 informs us, ...***without faith*** *it is impossible to please God, because anyone who comes to him must believe that he exists and that he rewards those who earnestly seek him.* Seek God and believe He will reward you.

Unhealthy attachments to things can make you greedy. You will know you are greedy when you fear losing things. That fear leads to the dark side, because you begin to search for the power to keep hold of things. Those who hunger for righteousness are just the opposite. They are not attached to things or a certain way of life. They have discovered that life is empty and has no meaning without God. Things can come and they can go. Inevitably, it is all temporary. Whereas, God and the things of God are eternal. As we hunger for righteousness, we are satisfied, as long as God is going before us and is with us.

In Romans 6:21-22 Paul admonishes the Christians in Rome saying, *What benefit did you reap at that time from the things you are now ashamed of? Those things result in death! But now that you have been set free from sin and have become slaves to God, the benefit you reap leads to holiness and the result is eternal life.* The benefit of being freed from the bondage of sin is holiness.

Happy people are content with whom God has made them to be, and with the life He has given them to live. Yet, I want to point out that this doesn't mean they are complacent. They do still desire to have more of God. They will still be seeking out Bible studies, teachings and ways to learn more about God, and how to progress in their spiritual formation. They are not satisfied to think that they have attained all that there is to attain. They know there is more and they hunger for it.

As Christians, we should desire to continually grow spiritually. The great thing is, as we hunger and thirst for God, He Himself satisfies our hunger, as with the richest of spiritual food. He satisfies us with His very Presence and we feel, "so satisfied." (Psalm 63:5) Yet I desire more of Him today than yesterday, because I see that there is more of Him that I have not yet experienced. Psalm 90:14 tells us that God satisfies us with His unfailing love. Spending time with God and allowing Him to be our Source for all we need in life is the only way to experience genuine satisfaction. He is the Fountain of Living Waters. If you have been seeking for satisfaction in other places, repent and turn from those broken cisterns. God declared in Jeremiah 2:13, *My people have committed two sins: They have forsaken me, the spring of living water, and have dug their own cisterns, broken cisterns that cannot hold water.* People, positions, rewards, fame and fortune are all broken cisterns. Although they may bring a temporary lift, it soon fades and we find ourselves in search for more. Our souls are never truly satisfied unless we seek God and determine to walk uprightly before Him. It is in this place we experience real satisfaction.

I also want to point out that those who hunger and thirst for righteousness, do not hunger only to see God's ways at work in their own lives, but also to see His righteousness flourish within the church and in the world. They desire to honor God by fearing the Lord and keeping His commandments. When we see a lack of godly reverence in our world, as those who hunger for righteousness, we grieve. Yet, we are motivated to carry on as we discover our satisfaction in Christ.

The Blessing: Satisfaction, fulfillment

The Recipient: Those who desire and pursue God and His ways

Jesus said to them, I am the bread of life; he who comes to Me will not hunger, and he who believes in Me will never thirst.
–John 6:35 NASB

Reflect and Grow:

Resulting spiritual fruit: Patience

Characterization of the meek: Spends time with God; is calm, even-tempered, self-controlled, and able to tolerate delay

Opposite worldly attitude: Self-centered, quick tempered, unsatisfied

Opposing worldly value: Pursuit of personal needs & self-gratification

1. Consider the spiritual fruit produced when you cultivate this attitude. Think of a Scripture that you can sow as seed at times the opposite attitude tries to take root in your heart.

2. Notice the opposite worldly attitude. Compare this to Galatians 5:19-21. Are you being influenced by any of these ungodly vices?

3. Look at the characterization listed above for this beatitude and compare it to its opposing worldly value. How do they differ? Compare the opposite worldly attitude above with the one who hungers for righteousness. What area(s) or circumstance in your life exists that you need to make an intentional decision to lay down the

worldly value and/or attitude to pick up the character trait of this beatitude?

4. To develop this attitude: Consider John 16:5-11; Philippians 3:7-11.

Things to Remember:

- Ask God to fill you with His love.
- Pray that God will increase your desire for Him (Ask, believing, and you will receive).
- Be intentional to do the following even if you do not feel like it. If you will do these things, your desire for God and His ways will increase:
  - Set time aside to spend in The Word of God.
  - Meditate on Scripture and allow God to speak to you through it.
  - Spend time in prayer.
  - Bring to remembrance all the things in your life you have to be thankful for and thank God for His faithfulness in your life.
  - Spend time in worship, corporate and when you are alone.
  - Ask God to take control of your life.

Seek and Apply:

Attitude Check-up: To examine your life for meekness, ask yourself:

1. Do you fear the loss of those you love—parents, husband, children? The loss of material things? The loss of position?

2. Do you have a hunger and thirst for God, desiring to know Him and His ways more intimately? If so, what are you doing to grow in that

intimacy? Read Proverbs 8:17. What does this verse suggest we can do to grow in intimacy with God?

3. You can go to God in faith and ask Him to give you a love for Him. How does 1 John 5:14 support this statement?

4. Read Luke 10:27, *'Love the Lord your God with all your heart and with all your soul and with all your strength and with all your mind' and, 'Love your neighbor as yourself.'* What does it mean to you to Love God with your heart? Your soul? Your strength? Your mind?

5. Do you seek after attention and acceptance from others? Sometimes even to your own detriment? How might seeking God instead, take care of this need?

6. What are you turning to in order to fill a void in your soul? Has it filled you or left you feeling empty again?

7. Are you working overtime, striving for promotion to make yourself feel good about yourself? If so, is it working? Why or why not? What can you do to increase your love and acceptance of yourself?

8. What does it look like to love God with your heart, soul, strength and mind in everyday life? Ask Him to give you this kind of love for Him! What does it look like to love your neighbor? What does James 4:2b tell us is the reason we lack what we need?

9. What are the two types of righteousness in the Bible? What are the differences between them?

10. What does it mean that we legally have a right standing before God?

11. Pray and then set some goals as to what you might do in your journey to seek to live uprightly before God. Start with some small goals that are doable and then after 30 days, you may want to add to your efforts.

> *"May the Lord diect your hearts into God's love and Christ's perseverance"*
> —2 Thessalonians 3:5

Prayer

Father, I repent for seeking satisfaction in people, things and positions. Stir up within me a hunger and thirst for righteousness. I thank You that I can come to You freely and You will satisfy my hunger and thirst. Lord, You satisfy my soul every morning with Your loving kindness (PS 90:14). Thank You for satisfying me with The Living Word, Jesus Christ, and Your written Word which is Spirit and Life. I thank You that, as I seek You and Your ways through Bible study and prayer, I am transformed. You satisfy my soul to the fullest, as if satisfied with an abundance of food and living water, never to hunger or thirst again. In Jesus' name, Amen.

You're blessed when you care. At the moment of being 'care full,' you find yourselves 'cared for.'

–Matthew 5:7 MSG

Chapter Ten

The One Who Cares is Cared For

In verse 7 of Matthew Chapter 5, we see that *the one who is happy, to be envied, and spiritually prosperous—with life-joy and satisfaction in God's favor and salvation, regardless of the outward conditions* is "the one who cares." As you show mercy, you receive mercy. The Message Bible states that as you are *care full* (that is, full of care for others), you find yourself *cared for* by God.

The Greek word used in this beatitude for merciful, was taken from the Greek word, "eleemon." Eleemon is a kind, compassionate, sympathetic, merciful and sensitive word, combining tendencies with action. A person with this quality finds outlets for his merciful nature. Charitable, philanthropic relief finds its origin in this word.[18] In other words, giving mercy towards those who are not able to give anything in return is walking as a merciful servant of God. Jesus calls us to an attitude of mercy that goes even beyond our everyday interactions.

Let's pause for a moment and enjoy a little humor to lead us into our exploration of this beatitude— A young lady, who occasionally walked through the park after work, stopped one day to have her picture taken by a photographer. She was very excited about her picture being taken. As she walked out of the park, she looked at the Polaroid picture in total amazement. She turned and headed back to the photographer. When she got there, she said, 'This is not right! This is not right! You have not done me justice!' The photographer looked at the picture and looked at her and stated, 'Miss, you don't need justice, what you need is mercy.'[19]

Okay, you may be thinking that was not all that funny, but it is a good story to help us understand the character trait 'mercy.' I have heard our pastor, Michael Fletcher, say, so many times, "We do not want God to deal with us justly. What we want is mercy!" If God dealt with us justly, none of us would be here today.[20] Sometimes we think we look pretty good, but if we stop and really look into our hearts where God is checking us out, justice is not what we want. The following story gives us another look into mercy:

> "A mother once approached Napoleon, seeking a pardon for her son. The emperor replied that the young man had committed a certain offense twice and justice demanded death.
>
> "But I don't ask for justice," the mother explained. "I plead for mercy."
>
> "But your son does not deserve mercy," Napoleon replied.
>
> "Sir," the woman cried, "it would not be mercy if he deserved it, and mercy is all I ask for."
>
> "Well, then," the emperor said, "I will have mercy."
>
> And he spared the woman's son.[21]

Mercy gives something good to those who do not deserve it. In addition to extending merciful acts to those who may not be involved with our lives on a personal level, we should also have as our goal to be a person who is merciful towards those in our daily interactions. In fact, perhaps this is a good place to begin to cultivate this virtue.

When you are walking in mercy toward another, you do more than pray for them; you begin to walk in that person's shoes, empathizing with their experience. You ask questions, because you want to understand what they are experiencing, so you can help in some way. You may ask your friend, "I understand you are struggling. Is there anything I can do to help?" "What has happened? Do you know the root cause of your behavior, addiction, etc.?" You want to know because you care. Recognizing your own weaknesses and sin nature, you are able to deal gently with those who are lacking knowledge or are going astray. Just as we need and expect so much mercy from God and others, so we must be willing to show mercy to others.

Scripture tells us that Jesus was a man of sorrows. Hebrews 4:15 says, *For we do not have a high priest who is unable to sympathize with our weaknesses, but we have one who has been tempted in every way, just as we are—yet was without sin.* I am so glad that Jesus did not leave me in my sin! Jesus understands and extends His mercy to me. He walks with me through my troubles, and He wants me to walk through troubles alongside others. He wants me to give support and encouragement to those who are struggling and allow the Holy Spirit to mend and heal the brokenhearted in His way and in His timing. He wants you to do this too.

Just as we need and expect so much mercy from God and others, so we must be willing to show mercy to others.

There are times that others may really mess up with us. They may be having a challenging day, experiencing physical pain or they may be struggling with a personal issue such as finances or family problems. It could be that they just didn't get enough rest the night before. Whatever the reason, they may respond or lash out in a hurtful way. I am sure you have acted inappropriately at some time yourself. I know I have. The person who cares for others will forgive and go on recognizing their need for forgiveness. We don't always know what kind of stress another person is undergoing, and we don't know that we wouldn't need the same kind of grace shown towards us. We need to remember that both we, and the one asking for forgiveness, are sinners saved by grace, and, thus, sometimes have a difficult time handling the stress of life. This, my friends, is the way of grace. This is the grace God has shown us as He reconciled us to Himself, even though we were at enmity against Him.

When it comes to forgiving others, The Scripture is very clear that we must do it in order to receive forgiveness ourselves from God (See Matthew 6:14, 15). In fact, according to Matthew 18:21, 22 we will need to do this repeatedly and frequently. It's amazing how eager we are to accept God's forgiveness seventy times seven for the same wrong we have committed against God; yet we are oftentimes stingy in extending any mercy at all towards someone who has offended us. These attitudes will stop up the free flow of His grace and power while releasing the flow of sleeplessness, sickness, bitterness and other such things in your life. These are the torturers spoken of in Matthew 18. Here Jesus shares a story in verses 22-35 that depicts the seriousness of allowing unforgiving attitudes to remain in our lives. I suggest you read this parable and meditate on it. In this story, the King (God) forgives a servant (you and I) of a huge debt owed to him. Then the servant turns around and refuses to forgive a small debt owed him by one of his servants (the one who has hurt or offended you or I). The story ends with the King's judgment against this unforgiving servant, He says to him in verse 32-34, Then the master called the servant in. *'You wicked servant,' he said, 'I canceled all that debt of yours because you begged me to. Shouldn't you have had mercy on your fellow servant just as I had on you?' In anger his master turned him over to the jailers to be tortured, until he should pay back all he owed.* Then in verse 35 we read, *This is how my heavenly Father will treat each of you unless you forgive your brother from your heart.*

Spiritual health is being able to release forgiveness towards others, knowing that they are just like you, a person at times influenced by the effects of the fall—a sinner in need of mercy. It is being able to walk in God's presence and enjoy Him ourselves, yet still feel the hurts of people around us who do not know Him or are feeling far away from Him. As we walk in mercy toward others, we receive mercy from our heavenly Father, and we experience the blessed, happy life available to those who belong to God.

Another important principle we need to employ in our lives is that of not comparing ourselves to others or others to ourselves. It is difficult to maintain an attitude of caring when comparing. If you compare yourself to others, it will either result in pride or feelings of unworthiness. There is always someone who is walking in more maturity than we are ourselves yet there is also someone who hasn't yet experienced the depth of relationship with God that we have. 2 Cor 10:12 explains, *We do not dare to classify or **compare** ourselves with some who commend themselves. When they measure themselves by themselves and **compare** themselves with themselves, they are not wise.* Galatians 6:4 NCV reads, *Each person should judge his own actions and not **compare** himself with others. Then he can be proud for what he himself has done.*

Jesus Christ is our only standard of measurement, and, when we compare ourselves to Him, we always fall short of the glory of God. There is no room to boast. But we also know that we have the mercy of God available to us as we repent of our sins (1 John 1:9). People desperately need to experience the mercy of Christ through those of us they can see. I have had times in my life, and will most likely have more, when I need people to walk in mercy towards me.

God again, in James 2:13, stresses the importance of the existence and exercise of this attitude in our lives, *Judgment without mercy will be shown to anyone who has not been merciful. Mercy triumphs over judgment!* Martin Luther said, "What is it to serve God and to do His will? Nothing else than to show mercy to our neighbor. For it is our neighbor who needs our service; God in heaven needs it not."[22]

Walking with an attitude of mercy towards others when they "mess up" with us or with someone else, is a demonstration of love. Love is at the very foundation of our walk with the Lord. Scripture tells us that without love, it doesn't matter what else we are doing in the Kingdom. 1 Cor 13:1-7 puts it this way, *If I speak in the tongues of men and of angels, but have not love, I am only a resounding gong or a clanging cymbal. If I have the gift of prophecy and can fathom all mysteries and all knowledge, and if I have a faith that can move mountains, but have not love, I am nothing. If I give all I possess to the poor and surrender my body to the flames, but have not love, I gain nothing. Love is patient, love is kind. It does not envy, it does not boast, it is not proud. It is not rude, it is not self-seeking, it is not easily angered, it keeps no record of wrongs. Love does not delight in evil but rejoices with the truth. It always protects, always trusts, always hopes, always perseveres.*

If we are not living with a loving attitude towards people, yet think we are walking a godly walk, we are deceiving ourselves. Christ told us that the whole law hung on two commands. Those two commands are, to love God and to love others. They are found in Matthew 22:37-40, *'Love the Lord your God with all your heart and with all your soul and with all your mind.' This is the first and greatest commandment. And the second is like it: 'Love your neighbor as yourself.' All the Law and the Prophets hang on these two commandments.*

There are times people will look upon others—what they say, what they do—and judge them. They will begin talking about that person and brand them as being difficult or short-tempered, angry or in need of emotional healing, just because of one incident—one weak moment in their life. We need to guard ourselves from judging others at all times. We do not know what the circumstances might be in that person's life at any moment. Even if you could walk in their shoes, you really couldn't because although your circumstances are the same, your emotional and psychological makeup is unique, as is theirs. The influence and effect of what appears to be the same circumstantial challenge will affect each of us differently. As Christians, representing Christ in the world, we must become more diligent to guard ourselves from judging others.

If you have been one who judges, instead of extending mercy, repent of this sin and begin today to show mercy towards others. I promise you, you have been in need of the same mercy, and God has granted it to you. You need mercy yourself not only from God, but also from people in your life. If not now, just wait, you will. Remember, only God qualifies to judge. He intricately formed each of us in our mother's womb, including the person you are judging! Only God knows the road they have traveled and how their life experiences have affected them. He knows every place that needs healing, every place that needs repentance, and He alone can shepherd them into a place of wholeness and righteousness. He alone can judge righteously.

The Blessing: Receives care and mercy from God and others

The Recipient: Those who offer mercy and display care towards others

For if you forgive others for their transgressions, your heavenly Father will also forgive you.

–Matthew 6:14

Experience Godliness God's Way

Reflect and Grow:

Resulting spiritual fruit: Kindness

Characterization of the merciful: Merciful in their interactions with others, demonstrate God's heart of forgiveness as well as extend practical help to those who are in need, both within and outside of their daily interactions

Opposite worldly attitude: Lack of love and obedience to God; revengeful; seeks justice for self

Opposing worldly value: Strength without feeling; religious rituals

1. Consider the spiritual fruit produced when you cultivate this attitude. Think of a Scripture that you can sow as seed at times the opposite attitude tries to take root in your heart.

2. Notice the opposite worldly attitude. Compare this to Galatians 5:19-21. Are you being influenced by any of these ungodly vices?

3. Look at the characterization listed above for this beatitude and compare it to its opposing worldly value. How do they differ? Compare the merciful with the opposite worldly attitude. What area(s) or circumstance in your life exists that you need to make an intentional decision to lay down the worldly value and/or attitude to pick up the character trait of this beatitude?

4. To develop this attitude: Consider John 16:5-11; Philippians 3:7-11.

Things to Remember:

- It's difficult to care when you compare.
- God alone can judge righteously.
- Those who call their walk godly, yet withhold love from others, are deceived.

- We all need mercy, not justice.
- Mercy gives something good to those who do not deserve it.
- Those who withhold mercy and forgiveness will have mercy and forgiveness withheld from them.

Seek and Apply:

Attitude Check-up:

1. Who do you use as your standard of measurement for your life and why?

2. What is the first and great commandment? How does this relate to the attitude studied in this chapter? How can you show your love for God? For others?

3. Who have you been quick to judge whose weakness may be different than your own? Repent and ask God to help you extend mercy towards them.

4. If you are walking in love, showing mercy toward others, as our Father has shown mercy towards you, how is this being displayed? What does this look like in real practical living? Consider God's mercy in light of Matthew 18:22-35.

5. Think of a time when you needed others to have grace towards you, and they did. What effect did their display of grace have on you? Think of a time when grace was withheld. How did that affect you? How might your giving mercy towards another affect their life? Think about the affect it might have in light of eternity.

6. When others stumble, or are in times of trial, how could you show compassion towards them? Is there anyone in your life right now who needs to know they are cared for? Is there something you can do to relate your care for them?

7. Are you concerned about those who do not know Jesus? How is this seen in your actions? What can you do this year to reach at least one for Christ?

8. Think about your friends, your church and your community. Pray and ask God what you might be able to do to show His love for them. Is there someone in your community you have in your power to touch with the mercy and love of God? Who could you touch with God's mercy who is not in a position to do anything in return for you?

9. Read Hosea 6:6. What is God speaking to you through this verse in regards to mercy and care for others?

10. Memorize and ask God to imprint the Truth of Ephesians 2:4-5 into your mind and soul, "But because of his great love for us, God, who is rich in mercy, made us alive with Christ even when we were dead in transgressions—it is by grace you have been saved."

Continue to think of ways that you can give this kind of mercy towards others.

Father, I commit to be an imitator of You. You showed mercy towards me even when I did not deserve it, and You continue to do so day by day. Help me to walk in love as Christ has loved me and given Himself for me, an offering and a sacrifice to You for a sweet-smelling aroma (Eph 5:1-2). Lord, I thank You that my mercy shown towards others is also pleasing to You and because I forgive others, I know that You also forgive me. In Your name, Amen.

God blesses those whose hearts are pure, for they will see God.

–Matthew 5:8 NLT

Chapter Eleven

Cultivating a Passion for Purity

God calls us His children now. This fact, coupled with the knowledge that God loves us, gives us our self-worth. Knowing that we are His children should encourage us to cultivate an attitude of purity so that we may experience an increasingly intimate relationship with God, our Father.

Since we have these promises, dear friends, let us purify ourselves from everything that contaminates body and spirit, perfecting holiness out of reverence for God (2 Corinthians 7:1).

Hebrews 12:14 says, *Make every effort to live in peace with all men and to be holy; <u>without holiness no one will see the Lord</u>* (Emphasis by Author). The *New American Standard* version says ...*without sanctification no one will see the Lord.* The Jews were required to go through a ceremonial cleansing ritual to symbolically cleanse themselves of their sins before entering the Temple where God's presence dwelt. Sin creates a barrier between us and God and although He is with us, we are unable to see Him. If we want to experience an intimate relationship with God, we must renounce our sin and commit to obey Him. We also must put away deceit and lying. Deceit hinders any relationship. Thus, in order to have ongoing communication between ourselves and God requires that we tear down any walls of dishonesty and self-deception (PS 24:3-4).

> What can we do to accelerate the development of this attitude in our lives?
>
> For one thing, we need to pray regularly. Psalm 19:12-13 cries out to God,
> *Forgive my hidden faults.*
> *Keep your servant also from willful sins; may they not rule over me.*
> *Then will I be blameless, innocent of great transgression.*

In Psalm 51:10, David asks God, *Create in me a clean heart, O God, And renew a steadfast spirit within me.* David realized that when he sinned with Bathsheba by taking another man's wife, he had followed his natural inclination to please himself rather than to please God. This is true of all of us when we sin. We are choosing to satisfy our sinful nature at the expense of God's presence. We can follow David's example here and ask God to clear our hearts and spirits of ungodly thoughts and make room for pure ones. We also pray for God to give us an open heart to receive conviction of sin and an obedient spirit to be quick to repent of it.

In addition to praying, we need be diligent to filter our hearts. Proverbs 4:23 reads, *Above all else, guard your heart, for it is the wellspring of life.* We need to guard what we allow to enter into our hearts through the gateway of our senses, especially our eyes and our ears. Be particular about what you choose to look at and what you choose to listen to. Again using King David as an example, when he stood on his rooftop and looked out onto Bathsheba's balcony where she was bathing, he could have guarded himself by immediately turning away and leaving the place where he had such a view. If you are prone to temptation with pornography, you should have protections on your computer. If you struggle with any kind of ungodly temptation, show your genuine desire for godliness by putting guard posts in place for your protection. It is a good idea for all believers to have someone in their lives to hold them accountable even in their attitudes.

Another necessary thing we must do to grow in an attitude of purity and become a reflection of Christ is to read Scripture and allow the Word to get into our hearts. Remember we reap what we sow. When we sow Jesus (the Word) we reap His life through ours. The Word of God is the seed we sow, and, the more we sow, the more harvest of God's purity we will reap. *Do not let this Book of the Law depart from your mouth; meditate on it day and night, so that you may be careful to do everything written in it. Then you will be prosperous and successful* (Joshua 1:8). Meditating is more than a quick reading and checking another item off your list for the day. According to J.I. Packer, meditating has to do with turning your knowledge about God into knowledge of God. In his book, <u>Knowing God</u>, Packer states, "Meditation is the activity of calling to mind, and thinking over, and dwelling on, and applying to oneself, the various things that one knows about the works and ways and purposes and promises of God." He further says, "Its purpose is to clear one's mental and spiritual vision of God, and to let his truth make its full and proper impact on one's mind and heart."[23] Knowledge of the Word alone, without meditation and the Spirit's illumination will result in puffing us up. Therefore, be sure to invite the Holy Spirit to illuminate the heart of God to you while meditating on His Word. 1 Corinthians 8:1b, *Knowledge puffs up, but love builds up.*

We can also cooperate with God in transforming our attitudes by speaking to our selves. But be careful—our fallen human tendency is to listen to our un-renewed self rather than talk to our self as led by the Word of God. We want to make sure we are sowing the right kind of seed and not seed from thoughts contrary to God that are attempting to take root within us. Follow the example David gives us in Psalm 42:5, 11, *Why are you downcast, O my soul? Why so disturbed within me? Put your hope in God, for I will yet praise him, my Savior and my God.* We need to encourage ourselves and even command ourselves to obey God in this same way .

If you are to progress in an attitude of purity, it is also imperative that you learn to train your mind to think about Jesus, refusing to give place to any thought that comes your way that is at cross purposes to the Word of God. 2 Corinthians 10:3-4 NASB states, *Though we walk in the flesh, we do not war according to the flesh, for the weapons of our warfare are not of the flesh, but divinely powerful for the destruction of fortresses.* As I mentioned earlier, Paul commands us in 2 Timothy to train ourselves in godliness. We train ourselves and we tear down the fortresses of the enemy by using the weapons and tools God has provided us—prayer, faith, hope, love, the Word of God and the indwelling Holy Spirit. There is no method or strategy we can come up with that works like these weapons do.

2 Corinthians 10:5 goes on to remind us of the importance of surrendering even our thought life to the sovereign control of Almighty God. We read, *we are destroying speculations and every lofty thing raised up against the knowledge of God, and we are taking every thought captive to the obedience of Christ.* We must take our thoughts captive and allow only those thoughts that agree with the Word of God to freely flow through our minds. We need to take our thoughts captive and command ourselves what to think.

I determined a number of years ago that I wanted God to be my first thought each morning. I wanted to be aware of His presence throughout my day, no matter what activity I was involved. I asked God to help me increase my awareness. When I first open my eyes in the morning, I immediately say "Good morning, Father. Thank you for this day. You have made it and I will rejoice and be glad in it." I pray each night before I sleep and, yes, I tell my Lord and Savior good night, just as I tell my husband or my children good night. I speak out loud to Him. This begins and ends the day right, and I continue the practice throughout the day. The practice of practicing His presence increases our awareness of His holiness standing before us. Whatever I am thinking upon or doing, instead of talking to myself, I talk to God. When I stop talking, I hear His voice in my spirit. I have found this to be a great way to train my mind to think upon Jesus throughout the day. You can choose to consciously and intentionally increase your awareness of Him in this way.

> *We must take our thoughts captive and allow only those thoughts that agree with the Word of God to freely flow through our minds.*

What do you do when impure, unclean thoughts enter your mind? Sometimes these thoughts seem to come out of nowhere. You could say the mind is a battleground, where thoughts battle to see which will take the ground and stake claim to our lives. How can you win this war? One important weapon against evil thoughts is to learn how to produce a counter-thought. A counter-thought is a powerful thought that provokes an image in the mind that opposes the ungodly one. The more powerful the corrupt image or thought, the more powerful the counter-image must be to counteract the unwanted mental impression. This counter thought must be directly from the Word of God.

If you have an area that you struggle with, I suggest you find Scriptures that you can use to directly deal with that particular challenge. Write these down on 3 x 5 cards. When these unwanted thoughts come to mind, you can pull out these cards and begin to speak the Word of God to the ungodly thought, just as Jesus did when undergoing His wilderness temptation that followed His water baptism in the Jordan River (Matthew 4). For instance, if you struggle with judgmental thoughts, then you might develop a set of 3" x 5" index cards on which you write scripture and references that will serve as counter-thoughts for those thoughts of judgment towards another. Perhaps you will even want two sets of scriptures—one set to remind you of your own sin and the judgment you deserved but did not receive from Jesus; and another set to remind you of the awesome fact that God Himself has not judged you, but has shown mercy towards you. Next, develop a mind picture to go along with these Scriptures. Pictures speak powerfully to our minds, and, when coupled with the Word of God, pictures will help you counter any thought that comes to war with your mind. Romans 12:2 instructs us, *Do not conform any longer to the pattern of this world, but be transformed by the renewing of your mind. Then you will be able to test and approve what God's will is—his good, pleasing and perfect will.*

I value using strong mental images of The Word of God to battle against opponents that wage war against us in our mind. Again, the stronger the opposing thought, the stronger this biblical image must be. I have heard the following recommendation from several pastors and I have found it to be very helpful…

Type a description of the horror that Jesus Christ underwent at Calvary, as described in His Word; then meditate on it until the picture is seeded in your mind, ready to be called to remembrance at any time. Within the first five to six seconds of the temptation, take your thoughts captive and demand of your mind to look steadfastly at the crucified form of Jesus Christ.

Let's say you just had a sexual thought that was inappropriate. Remember, you are in a war and your mind is the battlefield. Time is of the essence! You have seconds to keep from being overtaken by the enemy.

Speak to the ungodly thoughts and command them to depart from your mind. Next, call out to God, "God I need you. Help me!" Then demand of your mind, according to Romans 8:13, to fix its gaze on Christ on the cross. We have the authority to command our minds. Now remember that although Christ was God, He was also fully man. Therefore, He experienced and endured the excruciating pain that would accompany such a horrifying death.

According to Matthew Henry's Commentary, crucifixion was "so miserable a death that merciful princes appointed those who were condemned to it by the law, to be strangled first, and then nailed to the cross." *After studying what happened to Christ at Calvary, you should be able to visualize what He must have experienced that day.*

For example, your description may be something like this:

> Soldiers are mocking and spitting upon Him. He is gasping for breath causing His body to move up and down against the rough, wooden cross beam. Splinters are seen in the lacerations caused from the beating He received. The pain is intolerable and He cries out. He tries to pull away from the wood and the massive spikes through His wrist rip into the nerve endings. He screams again with agony and pushes up with His feet to give some relief to His wrists. His pain is intensified even more as the bones and nerves in His pierced feet crush against each other. He screams again in anguish. His throat is dry and raw. He thirsts but there is no relief. He cries out again; forgetting about the crown of two-inch thorns, He throws his head back in desperation only to hit one of the thorns perpendicular against the cross beam driving it half an inch into His skull. His voice reaches a soprano pitch of pain while blood flows down His body.

There He is at Calvary dying a bloody, cursed death of rejection, abandonment, shame and intolerable pain to pay the price to save you from your sin. I believe this same picture can be used for winning battles with gossip, envy, lust, lying, drunkenness or any other temptation. Every time you start to "go there again"—to your weak area of temptation, whatever it might be—go back to that powerful picture of Calvary. See Him there and make the choice that this sin will not be one that contributes to His suffering there.

Remember that there is no time in the spiritual realm, because time was created by God for man to live in. The eternal attribute of God indicates that God lives in one eternal present. Time has no affect on Him; He affects time. So when you consider that 2000 years ago and today are the same to God, you can see how bringing to your conscious mind a picture of the suffering of Jesus on the cross can be an effective deterrent to these attacks on our minds. Understand that I am not saying that Jesus is dying over again every time we sin. As discussed in a previous chapter, Christ paid an enormous price for my sin and the sins of all who call upon Him as Lord and Savior—past, present and future. No other sacrifice is needed or ever will be needed. God knew all the sins that those who Christ died for would ever commit, and He put it all on Christ that day at Calvary. Just before taking His last breath, Christ said, "It is finished." Therefore, when you sin and repent, you are appropriating the forgiveness and cleansing that Jesus paid for 2000 years ago at Calvary. However, seeing yourself right there before Him at Calvary, when you are about to commit sin, is a powerful deterrent. We are thankful that He paid the price for those sins we do commit. But because we love Him, we cannot bear, as we gaze upon Him on the cross, to allow the sin we struggle with today to be a part of the body of sin that caused His suffering then.

As you use this spiritual weapon in your battle against the temptations that wage war in your mind, you will find that you are no longer thinking about the sexual temptation or about how Susie should have and could have handled things differently. Besides, why do we always think our way is the only right way?

When you stand in your mind at Calvary and picture how it really was for Jesus because of your sin, because of the sin you are about to commit, you will be empowered to resist that sin and gain victory over it. The answer to overcoming temptation is found at Calvary.

When the day comes and we are face to face with Jesus, no other pleasure, and nothing of this life, will compare with the exhilaration of that moment! Nothing that goes on here on earth will matter to us at all! Nothing will ever mean so much as that opportunity of seeing God face to face. Nothing! That moment will be pure pleasure!

All believers carry with them a sin nature and a propensity to sin. It is dangerous for us to think we are "above" sinning as it is dangerous to minimize the consequence our sin can have in our relationship with God. Sin has the effect of blocking God's presence in our lives. We are called to resist the attraction of sin by the power of God that dwells in us. Yet, when we do sin, we are called to take responsibility for it, confess it openly to God and receive His forgiveness (1 John 1:9). He then restores us to a state of righteousness. This is God's way for us to walk in holiness.

Philippians 1:6 tells us that God began this good work in us and He will be faithful to complete it. However, we need to commit to cooperate with His work in our lives, and as we do, the fulfillment of our goal to be like Christ—living with a passion for purity, will be accelerated.

The Blessing: Evidence of God at work in all areas of life. See God increasingly more for who He is

The Recipient: The one who stays free from corruption of sin, by not living in a continual state of sin; one who upon realization of sin, quickly cleanses themselves through repentance

Who may ascend into the hill of the LORD?
And who may stand in His holy place?
He who has clean hands and a pure heart,
Who has not lifted up his soul to falsehood
And has not sworn deceitfully.

–Psalm 24:3-4

Reflect and Grow:

Resulting spiritual fruit: Goodness

Characterization of the pure: Has an intimate relationship with God cultivated through prayer, meditation and a study of His Word; Is transparent with God and others and seeks others for accountability in their attitudes and walk

Opposite worldly attitude: Immorality, life without boundaries

Opposing worldly value: Self-Deception; Deception with God and others

1. Consider the spiritual fruit produced when you cultivate this attitude. Think of a Scripture that you can sow as seed at times the opposite attitude tries to take root in your heart.
2. Notice the opposite worldly attitude. Compare this to Galatians 5:19-21. Are you being influenced by any of these ungodly vices?
3. Look at the characterization listed above for this beatitude and compare it to its opposing worldly value. How do they differ? Compare the pure at heart with the opposite worldly attitude. What area(s) or circumstance in your life exists that you need to make an intentional decision to lay down the worldly value and/or attitude to pick up the character trait of this beatitude?
4. To develop this attitude: Consider 1 John 3:1-3.

Things to Remember

- God will clear our hearts and spirits of ungodly thoughts and make room for pure ones, if we will ask.
- We must sow the pure thoughts into our minds. These pure thoughts will work to uproot the impure.
- Pray according to Psalm 51:10, *Create in me a clean heart, O God, And renew a steadfast spirit within me.*
- If we are serious about a passion for purity, we must take the responsibility to put guard posts in our lives. If we don't, we are not really serious.

On the road to purity you must:

Pray...

Focus on Christ's Triumph...

Guard the gateways of the heart...

Train your mind - Speak the Word of God aloud to yourself...

Take thoughts captive to the obedience of Christ...

In your mind, visit Calvary, remembering the price Christ paid for you to overcome sin.

Seek and Apply:

Attitude Check-up:

1. What worldly values clash with this attitude and your desire to walk in purity?

2. Read Ephesians 5:13. Why would it be difficult for someone to walk in purity if they are living a life void of transparency?

3. Read Psalm 24:3-4. Who will stand in the holy place? How does verse 4 describe a pure heart?

4. Have you memorized passages of Scripture that you can call upon in times of battle? Review them – or discover a few – then write them onto 3x5 cards and share with others.

5. Read 1 John 3:1-3. How does this passage encourage and instruct us in our desire to develop an attitude and lifestyle that reflects Christ in purity?

6. How long has it been since you meditated on Calvary? Think about and discuss how different your life and the world would be today had Christ fell to the temptation to walk away from His suffering? I want to encourage you to visit Calvary often. I believe it will deepen your relationship and commitment to godliness. Remember to ask God, as did David, Create in me a clean heart, O God, and renew a right, persevering, and steadfast spirit within me – (Psalm 51:10 AMP).

7. What can we do to help us make the right decisions, ones that are pure before the Lord? Read James 1:8 to help you formulate your answer.

8. Read Ephesians 6:10-17. What pieces of spiritual armor do you see that are available for every believer? How can each piece of this armor assist us in reaching our goal of 'purity'? What pieces of armor can you use for your current situation in order to conquer any impurity existing in your life?

9. How do we cleanse our conscience from guilt that we may stand before God? Read Hebrews 9:12-13,

10. Read Acts 15:8-9. How does God cleanse our hearts?

11. God is merciful. When you fall short, meditate on the following passage and thank God for His mercy and forgiveness.

If you are in a group study, read and discuss the following passage. How can you apply this to your life?

> *Although most of the many people who came from Ephraim, Manasseh, Issachar and Zebulun had not purified themselves, yet they ate the Passover, contrary to what was written. But Hezekiah prayed for them, saying, "May the LORD, who is good, pardon everyone who sets his heart on seeking God—the LORD, the God of his fathers—even if he is not clean according to the rules of the sanctuary." And the LORD heard Hezekiah and healed the people.*
>
> –2 Chronicles 30:18-20

Prayer

Father, thank You for Your gift of faith and your presence within empowering me for holy living. Create in me a clean heart and renew a right spirit within me. If there be any hidden agendas in what I do, please reveal them that I may repent and pursue You. Help me to be honest with myself and within my relationship with You and others. I desire inner holiness and to be faithful in every area of my life. I thank You to increase my love for you as I know when my love for You is greater than my love for sin, I will find the strength in You to refuse it. I thank You for the promise I have in 1 John 3:2 that when You appear I will be like You. In Your name, Amen.

God blesses those who work for peace, for they will be called the children of God.

–Matthew 5:9 NLT

Chapter Twelve

Children of God

What a great promise the above verse gives us, to be "children of God!" Of course, those who are born again became God's adopted sons and daughters at the time of their spiritual birth, but this Scripture is talking about character. Here Jesus tells us that we have our heavenly Father's "character" when we are peacemakers. It is talking about resembling our Father. If you want to look like your Daddy, then you will desire to cultivate this character trait in your life.

1 Corinthians 7:15 tells us that God has called us to live in peace. He desires us to show others how to cooperate and get along with one another, instead of how to compete and fight and see who can win the "I am right you are wrong" argument! As Christians, you would think that being a peacemaker would be right at the top of our priority list. Yet we at times find ourselves in the midst of friction in the church. Why is this? Why are there wars and rumors of wars? Why are people being killed and why are marriages being dissolved? Why are so many women and children suffering abuse, both physical and emotional? Almost everyone seems to be fighting for "their rights." People are betraying other people to get where they want and what they want! Yes,

unfortunately, even in the church. I have witnessed jealousy, false accusations, rumors and division many times between friends both in and outside of the church. It is unfortunate, but I have also seen a husband of one couple have an affair with the wife of another, in the same local fellowship. I have heard others tell their stories that have experienced the same divisive, self-focused behavior. I watched a young couple divorce after the wife had a brain tumor and as a result gained weight and required some additional grace in her healing process that the husband was not willing to give. What happened to "love and cherish in sickness and in health"? Why do these things happen except that we are looking inwardly, concerned about what we want, and what we think we deserve. This inward focus brings chaos and disorder into the lives of others as well as our own as we try to fulfill our selfish desires. Many times it results in damaging many people's lives. If we are to be peacemakers, we are going to have to learn to care for others' needs and trust God for our own.

My heart so cries out for unity within the body of Christ! I believe principles of conflict resolution, and teaching concerning what a peacemaker looks like, is desperately needed. After all, God says in Hosea 4:6 that His people are destroyed for lack of knowledge. People in general, and especially women, need to learn how to have disagreements with one another without it breaking their relationships. We need to be able to maintain peace even when we possess different opinions on various issues. We need to understand that you can still walk in unity, while having different perceptions and personalities. And although there may be times we have a heated disagreement, because of the one spirit of our Lord, we are enabled to reconcile. Therefore, if we are walking in the spirit of Christ, we should see more reconciliations and less permanent breaks in our relationships within the church. It is a choice we make, whether to continue in our flesh or walk in the spirit. We are enabled to make the right choice. All things are possible for those who are in Christ.

The Apostle Paul and Mark set a great example for us in the Book of Acts. In Acts 15 we read that Mark joined Paul and Barnabas on a missionary trip to Antioch. They preached in various cities along the way. Most people were probably intimidated by Paul. He had a reputation for persecuting the church yet after his conversion he developed a passion for the gospel that resulted in a tireless effort and boldness to share it. Many of his companions were not able to keep up with him.

We do not know what happened but we know that before the mission was complete, Mark returned to Jerusalem (Acts 13:13). Later Paul denied Mark the opportunity to join him on another trip because of his abandonment of this first mission. This resulted in Barnabas separating from Paul to take Mark on another outreach and Silas joined up with Paul as his new companion (Acts 15:37-39). What we need to recognize here is that personality differences may have played a large part of the rift that had developed between these men of God. Perhaps Mark was not ready for Paul's personality and aggressiveness and Barnabas would be able to teach him more than Paul at this point in time. But another key thing to recognize is that later passages reveal Paul nor Mark viewed this break as a permanent one. Also, Barnabas's recognition that Mark deserved a second chance resulted in this conflict becoming a growing experience for both Paul and Mark because eventually Mark grew into a trusted disciple and friend of Paul's. This means that Paul changed his perception concerning Mark. And Mark surely had to work through some issues concerning Paul's personality and way of dealing with him. They reconciled and became the best of friends. How did this happen? It happened because they were of one spirit and that spirit was the spirit of Christ.

The truth is, we are going to have disagreements; we are going to have misunderstandings. This is inevitable. Because we are all human beings in process, we will have misunderstandings until the day Christ comes for us or we go to Him, whichever comes first. That disputes will arise is not the issue. The issue is how we will handle those misunderstandings. There is no profit in becoming offended when everyone doesn't agree with us! Listen, disagreements do not give a reason to divide, withdraw or run away. As Christians, we are called to maintain a spirit of reconciliation at all times. Most disagreements are simple differences of opinions, and we should accept that each of us is going to have one. Disagreements can even be healthy. When handled in love, conflict can release creativity and new prayerfulness that births new ideas into a congregation or a relationship. Often it is a disagreement that brings to the surface deeper issues—matters that threaten the stability of the relationship if not dealt with.

There are times when a conflict needs to be entered into and issues need to be confronted, in order to resolve a situation that is causing a break. This is where the going gets tough. I have found this situation to be especially difficult for women, when it arises in the church. We find it difficult to balance the Biblical commands to forgive and forbear, with the need to speak up and confront. We ask, "How do we follow Christ and deal with conflict?" We wrongly think that we can't, so we run away from the relationship. I have had relationships that ended this way, and I have no idea what happened. I know I love the individuals, so why have they distanced themselves? I would not hurt anyone intentionally, but perhaps they perceived something I said or did in a way not intended. Perhaps they heard something that was untrue. Perhaps the difference in personalities, backgrounds, and/or experiences has influenced their conclusion on something I am unaware of. To avoid giving the enemy victory in these situations, it is imperative that we commit to communicate in our relationships. I believe most breaks can be avoided if we would stop sweeping our feelings under the rug and communicate with one another. If we truly love the individual who comes to us in this way, we are going to be so glad they have given us the opportunity to clear up the situation. We will apologize for any hurt that was experienced by them, due to any clumsiness on our part. At the same time, when we hear that someone we love has said something against us, or should someone offend us directly, we will go to them in an attempt to clear the air.

Life has taught many women to aim for "peace at any cost," but this attitude has resulted in much division in the body of Christ, whether seen in the natural realm or not. Women tend to be "peacekeepers" at the expense of "peacemaking." They think they are taking the low road by saying nothing, but there is a break left un-mended between the two individuals that has not been resolved. Because one or both of the individuals involved has stuffed the incident, refusing to talk and hear one another out, the individuals involved will drift further apart. The "stuffing it" solution is not the way of our Father. When there is a division at hand, we should not take on the attitude of "peacekeeping." God has called us to "peacemaking." There is a huge difference. Think about it. Does God stuff His feelings concerning matters? When you have done something to displease Him, does He walk away from you and completely abandon the relationship? Of course He doesn't. And we shouldn't either, because it doesn't glorify God, it isn't God's way and it doesn't profit anyone. It simply gives a resemblance of peace, but it is not the real thing. It is a selfish way to handle our conflicts, as the one walking away is concerned only about them self and maintaining their own peace by avoiding the person, thus avoiding the issue. The truth is, we are called to think of others more than ourselves. Should you walk away

When we become God-centered and we are bent on pursuing peace, then we are not so ruffled when someone disagrees with us.

from a relationship, the person, who is left, may suffer feelings of rejection and may even temporarily walk away from God. We need to think about others and the affect our actions may have on them. Mark 9:42 says, *And whoever causes one of these little ones (these believers) who acknowledge and cleave to Me to stumble and sin, it **would** be **better** (more profitable and wholesome) for him if a [huge] millstone were hung about his neck, and he were thrown into the sea.* This is a serious issue before God. Those who walk away are taking the road that is most comfortable for them at the expense of their relationship with God and the ministry of reconciliation believers are responsible to. They are walking away without concern of another's feelings or work with the Lord. This is not the way of love. This is not the way of Christ. For me, it is hurtful to lose a friend and have no idea why. How about you?

So why do we find it so difficult to be honest with one another and talk things out openly? When we were young, most of us had no problem speaking out about our feelings. However, as we approached junior high school, we discovered that speaking truth about our feelings caused us to lose a relationship or two. We learned to stuff our feelings or to run away, in order to avoid conflict and suffer rejection. The bottom line is that women tend to avoid conflict out of fear of rejection and ridicule. As Christian women, we deceive ourselves, get religious, and call it taking the low road. This is a serious problem we have in our lives and in our churches. The result is that relational disagreements and conflicts are constantly simmering below the surface, threatening to erupt at any moment.

When we become God-centered and we are bent on pursuing peace, then we are not so ruffled when someone disagrees with us. We can deal with it, because we have learned to be free in whom we are, and we are able to allow others to be themselves too, not expecting their personality to be just like ours. Our relationship doesn't require that they agree with us in word or actions. We are free to pursue a unity that is real and true, rather than superficial and artificial, because, from our hearts, we desire agreement with fellow Christians, based on God's Truth and not on anyone's personal opinion.

It is difficult for a peacemaker, when she is trying to walk in this kind of honesty with someone, who in order to avoid rejection, lives their life by the "stuffing it" and "keeping quiet" pattern. There are times that the other person is unable to hear her thoughts, without becoming even more offended, and the relationship is irreparably broken. For example, many years ago I had noticed a change in the behavior of a working associate towards me. There were a couple of distinct things that took place that really bothered me. I decided that

I needed to approach her and ask her if I had done something to offend her. My desire was to have the opportunity to apologize and make things right if I had hurt or offended her. I didn't want this break in our relationship to remain, one that came out of nowhere. Believe me; I was scared to confront her. Why? I was concerned that I might be rejected in doing so. Knowing that she knew about the rejections in my past, I questioned, "What if nothing is wrong, it is my imagination and she then thinks I am acting out of a need for attention or approval." It is amazing how we can talk ourselves out of the transparency and openness required for true unity and peace. I decided that our relationship was worth the risk of rejection. I decided it was selfish of me to just pretend as though everything was okay and lose the relationship because of my fear. This particular experience did not produce the result I was hoping for. She was unable to handle an honest exchange. She responded defensively which suggested my discernment was correct and there was something bothering her. Because she was unable to deal biblically with offenses that were separating us, we are now cordial with one another, but the intimacy we once shared is gone. The broken relationship grieves me, but since I have done all I can to reconcile, I can know that my relationship with God is intact and I must move on. Remember, the relationship with my friend was not broken by the confrontation; it was broken by a conclusion she must have come to about something she heard or saw that I was unaware of. Although I desired reconciliation, she was content to believe a lie and hold her offence rather than honestly talk it out with me.

I want to give you two words of caution here. Avoid the temptation to use personal struggles a friend has shared with you during a time of discussing issues between you. Sometimes women will do this, trying to prove that the other must be the one at fault. After all, they have shared with you that they have "issues." This is not peacemaking, but waging war.

Secondly, don't run to someone else, even a leader, to share your offence, when you haven't first talked it over with the offender. How can a third individual possibly know what this person has in their heart? Always speak directly to the person you are offended with before reaching out to others. Sometimes a third party is needed to help bring reconciliation. If you have spoken to the offender and reconciliation has not taken place, to go for help after that may be warranted, depending on the situation (Matthew 18:15-17). Not to first approach the one with whom you have the issue is, however, gossiping and can cause unwarranted and unfair negative opinions about a person. Especially if you have been around longer within a particular fellowship or organization. After all, the people you speak to are human and we all tend to defend our friends and people we have known the longest. When the offense is due to a misunderstanding, you can see how our enemy—the one who comes to steal, kill and destroy the believer and the church—can use it to destroy an individual and the ministry God has called them to.

It is unfair to share your perspective with a third party without the other person involved in the conflict having the same opportunity. When a third party is brought into the situation, it must be with the intention that they act as a mediator, hearing both parties with the hope to bring reconciliation. Sometimes our efforts for reconciliation do not work, as it didn't in the example I shared. But I can promise you that many more times than not, it will work. I give this rare example to give you an example of what to do, should it not work. You must move on in your relationship with Christ.

We must take the chance and pursue true peace and true reconciliation, because God has called us to be ministers of reconciliation, not keepers of the peace. God calls us to make peace a priority in our lives. We read in Ephesians 4:3, *Make every effort to keep the unity of the Spirit through the bond of peace.* We can be the one to take the initiative and seek after peace. Here are some steps we can take.

1. We can begin by standing in the gap and praying. Ezekiel 22:30 says, *I looked for a man among them who would build up the wall and stand before me in the gap on behalf of the land so I would not have to destroy it, but I found none.*

2. Once we have prayed, we can reach out by making a phone call; making contact and setting up a meeting.

3. Try to be as gentle and non-threatening as you can while explaining your desire to preserve your friendship.

4. Don't call until you have fully forgiven any offenses you have against them, so that your motives are pure, and there are no accusations in your heart.

5. If the other person refuses to seek reconciliation, then you have done what you can; and although this relationship may be lost, your relationship with God is intact. Continue to pray for them, and forgive them. Although it can be difficult, because of your love for that person, at that point you must move on and press forward, leaving the past behind.

6. Guard your heart that a spirit of rejection does not enter in to you because of the unwillingness of the other party to reconcile with you; and know that you have done all that you can do. Remember that "Christ also accepted us to the glory of God" (Romans 15:7) and His acceptance is the one that really counts! Trust God with the situation and the person. Place both in the hands of God.

There is a huge difference between a peacekeeper and a peacemaker. God calls us to be "peacemakers." A "peacekeeper" is a person who appeases through wimpy niceness and conflict avoidance. They pursue "peace at any cost," many times at the cost of trading an intimate relationship for a superficial one. Many times women pursue peace, even at the risk of compromising or hurting themselves and what they believe. This is not what God desires we do. As you seek to be a peacemaker, if an issue arises that you cannot let go of, even after much prayer and soul-searching, don't fall for the temptation to just "stuff it." Instead, take steps towards making genuine peace that a relationship will have the opportunity to grow upon. Otherwise, although there may be a resemblance of peace, the relationship will continue to deteriorate. Don't ignore the problem. Don't be a "peace at any cost" woman, or man, for that matter. Your relationship is broken; and to be truly reconciled, conversation must take place. There is no other pathway for reconciliation. And reconciliation is always our Father's will.

It is very difficult for me to form intimate relationships with people who are peacekeepers. You never know what is true in the relationship. Peacekeepers can be offended with you about something, and you will never know, unless you find out through the grapevine. Of course when you hear this way, more damage usually happens to the relationship. It is frustrating when you notice something is not right, but you do not know what it is. If only those we love and co-labor with would give one another the opportunity to make things right. Otherwise, we give the enemy an open door to divinely set us up for misunderstandings that result in division.

In contrast, I appreciate my friends confronting me when they are bothered by something. This honesty and openness is an act of love, and shows they value our friendship. They are showing me they are willing to invest their time and energy into our friendship. They are willing to assume the best about me, by giving me an opportunity to explain myself, or the situation. When an issue threatens to separate us, they give me an opportunity to talk through my perspective on the issue and to explain myself in the misunderstanding.

Sometimes it becomes the opportunity to recognize that I am wrong, and I am really thankful for the opportunity to recognize that and apologize to them. It then becomes a growing experience—an opportunity to improve in my relational skills. This is one of the ideas God has in putting us in families, both natural and spiritual. The interaction with one another, including the friction points, brings growth opportunities to us if we would only allow them to be. I am quick to give the same respect and love towards my friends, even though sometimes it feels uncomfortable to do so. This is the only way for a true, intimate friendship to develop that is truly transparent in nature. This is walking in love and grace. But it only works if both people are committed to God and the relationship, walking in the unity of the same spirit—the spirit of Christ—a spirit of peacemaking.

> *God has called us to be ministers of reconciliation, not keepers of the peace.*

This same principle is true for having a great marriage. All of us must have grace for, and walk in love with, one another. Relationships grow stronger and healthier, when there is a freedom to share your true feelings, even when they don't make complete sense and even when they are unjustified. This freedom to share is necessary in order to have a genuine reconciliation between two individuals.

To be the peacemakers that God has called us to be, we not only need to approach one another with our hurt feelings, but we need to allow others to approach us in the same way, receiving them in love, not judgment. When they do, you can discuss, apologize, explain any misunderstanding, and give assurance of your intentions, that you would never intentionally hurt them. I am assuming, of course, that this is the case. I personally would want to tell someone who approached me in this way how much I love them and assure them that I would do my best not to let this "same thing" happen again. I would appreciate that she revealed this tender area of her soul with me, trusting me as a friend and woman of God, making herself vulnerable to me not to reject her for it. When we approach conflict in this way, we actually come to know one another even better, and our relationship grows stronger. Because I love my friend and because I would then know more about her emotional makeup and personality, I would be careful to not hurt her in this same way again.

On the contrary, if we settle for a resemblance of peace to deter conflict, the relationship is damaged. It may be a crack that is hidden, but eventually that crack can turn into a permanent break. The two individuals will gradually drift apart. Jesus Christ redeemed us by shining truth (light) into the situation of our lives. If we are to redeem our relationships, light must be shed into them. A peacemaker will make a plea for peace, asking the parties to lay down their arms, soften their hearts, and believe that God is able to reconcile the relationship. The key is to allow Him the opportunity. 2 Corinthians 5:20 says, *we implore you on Christ's behalf: Be reconciled to God!* When we are at war with one another, our relationship with God is broken as well. I ask you, is it worth it? I think not.

We all have varying backgrounds, experiences and personalities, and sometimes our perspectives on a given incident are totally different. When we disagree with someone's thoughts, feelings or values, we need to enter into a discussion concerning the issue. We need to help them to see our view and be willing to listen to theirs. Sometimes it is not a matter of anyone being right or wrong. Both people can be right when you see it through the other's perspective, but to truly come to a place of reconciliation, this step cannot and must not be avoided. Some of you may have seen the picture that for some looks like a beautiful young woman but to others when they look at it, they see an old woman. It is a great example of how two people can see two different pictures when looking at an object or a situation. We can ask God to help us be open to see through one another's eyes in repairing broken relationships.

What do you see – young or old woman? Now try to see the other.

Of course, there are those times when we should just forgive and forbear. We see God's example of forbearance in Romans 3:25, *whom God set forth as a propitiation by His blood, through faith, to demonstrate His righteousness, because in His forbearance God had passed over the sins that were previously committed.* For example, we all have little idiosyncrasies that bother us, or that bother us when we see them in others. Sometimes our personalities, backgrounds and cultures have given us different perspectives, ways of talking and doing. Sometimes these things just have to be accepted about another, even though in our own personality, their actions rub us the wrong way. We continue on, by the grace of God. This, too, is a biblical principle and is seen in Colossians 3:13 AMP, *Be gentle and forbearing with one another and, if one has a difference (a grievance or complaint) against another, readily pardoning each other; even as the Lord has [freely] forgiven you, so must you also [forgive]*. In other words, I am not advocating that we bring up every little difference. That would alienate and cause even those who walk as peacemakers to avoid our presence.

But when a wounding seems to have taken place in your soul, then you need to talk. Or, when there appears to be a break in the relationship, you need to approach your friend. You might say something like, "I am bothered by something I heard the other day and would like to ask you about it." Or, "I am feeling hurt about something you said the other day and would like to ask you to share with me why you would say that or what you meant by that." If there appears to be a distancing, you may ask, "Is there anything wrong? Is there something that has come between us or is it just me?" When we are offended, most of the time, the person who offended us has no idea that they have done so. It is "simply a misunderstanding." What might be perceived as an intentional hurt is not what the person thought or intended at all. Learn to honestly communicate in love, and stop jumping to conclusions about situations and people. The pain you are experiencing could be instantly gone by having the light of the truth shed on the situation. And I reiterate, please don't be eager to run to others, including leadership, concerning the offense. Only the person(s) involved are able to shed true light and truth into the situation that concerns you, them and the situation at hand. Leadership should be deterring this kind of action, by simply asking the party coming to them, "Have you first gone to the offending party? If not, do that before making an appointment with me." Not instructing people in the biblical way causes much pain and sorrow and division in the body of Christ.

Another important part of this process is once we hear the other person's explanation, we need to be willing to receive it as truth and put away the perception we have been carrying that was breaking the relationship. We need to learn to forgive others for not being and acting in perfect harmony with us and with our ways of being and doing. I am convinced that a commitment to truthfulness, forgiveness and the giving of grace to one another is at the heart of walking in love and being a peacemaker. In one of my classes at Grace College of Divinity, we took various kinds of personality tests. One of the tests determined that my personality type is held only by 15% of the population. The test revealed how we process information. I immediately thought that this explains a lot about people and misunderstandings. If you are a person who processes information differently than 85% of the population, don't you think they may misunderstand you and you them? Thus, we see the need for commitment to talk things over in friendships and in co-laboring together for the advancement of the kingdom of God. God has uniquely formed us and we need to stop allowing the enemy to use our uniqueness as a tool to create division. We are now privy of his ways and know how to have victory over him.

Ken Sande, in his book "The Peacemaker" gives us a checklist to follow:

"Whenever you are involved in a conflict, you may apply the four basic principles of peacemaking by asking yourself these questions:

Glorify God: How can I please and honor the Lord in this situation?

Get the log out of your eye: How can I show Jesus' work in me by taking responsibility for my contribution to this conflict?

Gently restore: How can I lovingly serve others by helping them take responsibility for their contribution to this conflict?

Go and be reconciled: How can I demonstrate the forgiveness of God and encourage a reasonable solution to this conflict?"[24]

I will say it again, not speaking up to the "offender" as well as not listening to the "offended" causes the relationship to become fractured between the two parties, and not only between the two friends, but also between the offended and God. Do you hear what I am saying? It also causes the offended to have broken fellowship with God. Nothing is worth that! Do hear me. God will hold us responsible for adding to another's sorrow and pain that influences their relationship with Him. This is not just about you alone and your relationship. You are held accountable for your interactions with others. God loves peace and sends us into the world to mend broken relationships. It is time for the body of believers to grow up and approach conflict for the purpose of bringing light into the situation for healing and reconciliation. This is the way of love. This is the way of God.

To develop this character trait in our lives, we can follow the instruction found in Romans 12:9-21

> *Love must be sincere. Hate what is evil; cling to what is good. Be devoted to one another in brotherly love. Honor one another above yourselves. Never be lacking in zeal, but keep your spiritual fervor, serving the Lord. Be joyful in hope, patient in affliction, faithful in prayer. Share with God's people who are in need. Practice hospitality.*

Bless those who persecute you; bless and do not curse. Rejoice with those who rejoice; mourn with those who mourn. Live in harmony with one another. Do not be proud, but be willing to associate with people of low position. Do not be conceited.

Do not repay anyone evil for evil. Be careful to do what is right in the eyes of everybody. If it is possible, as far as it depends on you, live at peace with everyone. Do not take revenge, my friends, but leave room for God's wrath, for it is written: "It is mine to avenge; I will repay," says the Lord. On the contrary:

"If your enemy is hungry, feed him; if he is thirsty, give him something to drink.

In doing this, you will heap burning coals on his head." Do not be overcome by evil, but overcome evil with good.

As we learn to walk as peacemakers, we truly begin to resemble our Father as His "daughters" and "sons." Oh, my dear brothers and sisters in Christ, don't you want to hear Him say, 'that's my boy' or 'that's my 'girl'? "You're growing up and you sure do resemble your Daddy."

The Blessing: The special blessing of God as the Father blessing His child

The Recipient: Those who work for genuine peace: peacemakers versus peacekeepers

For all who are being led by the Spirit of God, these are sons of God.
–Romans 8:14

Reflect and Grow:

Resulting spiritual fruit: Faithfulness

Characterization of the peacemaker: Pursues peace at risk of rejection; is open and transparent in relationships; desires unity and reconciliation and is quick to offer forgiveness

Opposite worldly attitude: Argumentative; revengeful; peacekeeper

Opposing worldly value: Pursues personal peace without concern for others, or how their own actions may affect others

1. Consider the spiritual fruit produced when you cultivate this attitude. Think of a Scripture that you can sow as seed at times the opposite attitude tries to take root in your heart.
2. Notice the opposite worldly attitude. Compare this to Galations 5:19-21. Are you being influenced by any of these ungodly vices?
3. Look at the characterization listed above for this beatitude and compare it to its opposing worldly value. How do they differ? Compare the peacemaker with the opposite worldly attitude. What area(s) or circumstance in your life exists that you need to make an intentional decision to lay down the worldly value and/or attitude to pick up the character trait of this beatitude?
4. To develop this attitude: Consider Romans 12:9-21; Hebrews 12:10-11.

Things to Remember:

- In order to experience genuine inner happiness, one must be at peace with God and with people.
- God has not called us to be peacekeepers. He has called us to be peacemakers.
- Peacekeepers walk away from relationships when there is a rift instead of resolving the issue to bring about genuine reconciliation.

- Peacekeepers keep a resemblance of peace even at the cost of hurting others or even themselves.

- Peacemakers attempt to bring genuine reconciliation by bringing to light the issues that need to be resolved with the goal of restoring the relationship.

- Peacemakers do what's in their power to bring real peace. However, if the other party is not willing, they move forward knowing that their relationship is intact with God.

- There are times that we are called to simply forgive and forbear. These are the times when after prayer, we are able to let it go.

Seek and Apply:

Attitude Check-up:

1. Personal Reflection: Are you guilty of running from an uncomfortable conversation that needs to take place in order that your relationship may be reconciled? If so, why are you avoiding this conversation?

2. Think of an experience where you did "stuff it" and recall the outcome of the relationship.

3. Think of an experience where you confronted someone. What was the result? If it furthered the separation, how did you handle it? As you look back, can you see that the relationship would have been broken anyway?

4. Are you guilty of running to others to talk about offenses or relationship struggles (leadership or not leadership), under the pretense of getting counsel? Read Matthew 18:15-17. How can the instructions in this passage be applied to resolving the offenses in our lives? List the steps involved for resolving conflict as listed in this passage.

5. Read Psalm 103:6-14. How does this passage influence you in regards to developing the character trait of a peacemaker?

6. Read Proverbs 17:27. How can you apply this wisdom to your relationships?

7. Read Romans 12:14-21. What is Paul's advice to believers who are in conflict with those outside of the faith?

8. In 1 Corinthians 1:10, Paul pleads with the believers to be joined perfectly together in what? How can this be accomplished?

9. In Philippians 2:3, what attitudes are seen that result in disunity? What should we do to sow unity? (Philippians 2:3-4)

10. What action in Colossians 3:14 exhibits a mature spiritual character?

11. Read Colossians 3:2. What does it mean to "set your mind on things above"? How does this help you become a peacemaker? What are the things on earth that might compete for your affections and attention?

Prayer

Father, I thank You that You have made me a light on a hill that cannot be hidden. Let my light shine before men that they will see good deeds and praise You. Increase my longing for peace and help me to be one who helps others to achieve the same. I pray for a culture of peace in my church as well and that we may reflect the love and power of Christ. May You be glorified through us. In Jesus' name, Amen.

Blessed and happy and enviably fortunate and spiritually prosperous (in the state in which the born-again child of God enjoys and finds satisfaction in God's favor and salvation, regardless of his outward conditions) are those who are persecuted for righteousness' sake (for being and doing right), for theirs is the kingdom of heaven!

–Matthew 5:10 AMP

Chapter Thirteen

Happy and Favored While in the Midst of Persecution

When *your commitment to God provokes persecution,* Jesus tells us in this beatitude that you are blessed, and the persecution will drive you even deeper into God's kingdom! Then, just to make sure everyone understood exactly what He meant He added, *Blessed (happy, to be envied, and spiritually prosperous)… are you when people revile you and persecute you and say all kinds of evil things against you falsely on My account* (Matthew 5:11, AMP).

In other words, when you suffer persecution don't take it personally. It isn't about you. It is about the One who lives in you. These things happen in order to discredit Christ. It is about Him. The truth is, those who persecute you in this way are uncomfortable with you because the Truth dwells in you. Those walking according to the anti-Christ spirit are driven to destroy the character of God and all that belongs to Him. Their mission is to steal, kill and destroy (John 10:10).

Many times, Christians are persecuted, even by other Christians. Why does this happen? The Bible tells us there are three groups of people—those who are unbelievers, spiritually-minded believers, and carnally-minded believers. When we are spiritually minded, God and the things of God take priority in our life. Carnal minds are uncomfortable around those who live this way. In today's Christianity, in an attempt to walk free of religious man-made doctrines, many have confused carnal Christianity with godliness and perceive godliness as religiosity. We are warned of this very thing in Isaiah 5:20, *Woe to those who **call evil good** and **good evil**.* The godly person is one who has their mind focused on God. Religious people, on the other hand, have their minds focused on rules and regulations. Even if the motive was to eradicate religiosity, if your church has set up man-made ideas and rules one must follow to avoid being branded as a religious person, then you have become, yourself, a religious person. We need to detangle these ideas that result in judgmental attitudes.

When you are living with the truth reigning within your members, the darkness in people wants to hide. They feel like they are about to be exposed. You make them uncomfortable. Many times they do not understand or recognize your actions as being behavior that is led by the The Word of God, because they, themselves, are not living their lives in the Spirit. Matthew 5:12 AMP says, when you are being persecuted, you should, *Be glad and supremely joyful, for your reward in heaven is great (strong and intense), for in this same way people persecuted the prophets who were before you.* II Chronicles 36:16 says, *But they mocked God's messengers, despised his words and scoffed at his prophets until the wrath of the LORD was aroused against his people and there was no remedy.* James insinuates that the carnal Christian may persecute others, since their behavior is led by their ungodly thoughts. James 4:1-6 (MSG), *Where do you think all these appalling wars and quarrels come from? Do you think they just happen? Think again. They come about because you want your own way, and fight for it deep inside yourselves. You lust for what you don't have and are willing to kill to get it. You want what isn't yours and will risk violence to get your hands on it. You wouldn't think of just asking God for it, would you? And why not? Because you know you'd be asking for what you have no right to. You're spoiled children, each wanting your own way. You're cheating on God. If all you want is your own way, flirting with the world every chance you get, you end up enemies of God and his way.*

We don't find it easy to think about, but suffering does have a place in the life of a believer. Neither Jesus nor the Apostle Paul promised their followers a life of ease or public approval. In fact, what we see through their teachings is that those who do not belong to Jesus hate those who do. And as already mentioned, those who do belong to Him, but still love the things of the world, are uncomfortable around those who are fully surrendered to God. Jesus tells us in John 15:18-21, *If the world hates you, keep in mind that it hated me first. If you belonged to the world, it would love you as its own. As it is, you do not belong to the world, but I have chosen you out of the world. That is why the world hates you. Remember the words I spoke to you: 'No servant is greater than his master.' If they persecuted me, they will persecute you also. If they obeyed my teaching, they will obey yours also. They will treat you this way because of my name, for they do not know the One who sent me.*

Philippians 1:29 testifies, *For it has been granted to you on behalf of Christ not only to believe on him, but also to suffer for him.* In other words, suffering is a gift that comes to us, along with salvation. You may be thinking, but I don't want this gift. I just wanted to be saved. I understand that this is a difficult truth to comprehend. But think back to the commentary on the Book of Romans. When you received Christ, you became one with Him. Being one with Christ, how can those of the world love you when they hate Him? When we really grasp this, although we do not seek persecution, we understand it and that allows us to experience the blessing that is in it. Let's look at some more Scriptures.

Paul writes in Philippians 3:10, *I want to know Christ and the power of his resurrection and the fellowship of sharing in his sufferings, becoming like him in his death.* Paul has given us His example of how to respond to suffering and adversity, which come from the circumstances of life, in a way that transforms the adversity or suffering into glory. Jesus Himself is our supreme example. Romans 8:16-18 tells us that *we are co-heirs with Christ if, indeed, we share in His sufferings in order that we may also share in His glory.* I want to share in the glory of Christ. Don't you? Here God is telling us we cannot have one without the other. We read in 1 Peter 4:12-16, *Dear friends, do not be surprised at the painful trial you are suffering, as though something strange were happening to you. But rejoice that you participate in the sufferings of Christ, so that you may be overjoyed when his glory is revealed.* If you are insulted because of the name of Christ, you are blessed, for the Spirit of glory and of God rests on you. If you suffer, it should not be as a murderer or thief or any other kind

> *The persecution is a result of His glory resting on you. It is the spirit operating in your attackers that is persecuting you.*

of criminal, or even as a meddler. However, if you suffer as a Christian, do not be ashamed, but praise God that you bear that name. Are you getting this? If you have done nothing wrong—if you are loving people and walking uprightly before God, yet suffer even at the hand of the people who are supposedly your brothers and sisters in Christ, you can praise God. The persecution is a result of His glory resting on you. It is the spirit that is operating in your attackers that is persecuting you. What tremendous encouragement this knowledge should be to us.

It should not be strange to us, who are walking in the Spirit of Christ, to suffer persecution, insults and to have lies spoken against us. Suffering as a Christian goes along with bearing His name. Even Jesus was persecuted from within the institution, where the people gathered to worship God. We can be content in the midst of our suffering because:

- We know that as we share in His sufferings, we also will share in His glory.
- It is in suffering that the reality of our faith is made known to us.
- It is also in suffering that the power of the resurrected Christ is manifested in the life of the Christian for others to see and be drawn to Him.

We can also be content in our sufferings, knowing that such sufferings purify us, resulting in our becoming more like Christ. 2 Corinthians 4:11-18:

For we who are alive are always being given over to death for Jesus' sake, so that his life may be revealed in our mortal body. So then, death is at work in us, but life is at work in you.

It is written: "I believed; therefore I have spoken." With that same spirit of faith we also believe and therefore speak, because we know that the one who raised the Lord Jesus from the dead will also raise us with Jesus and present us with you in his presence. All this is for your benefit, so that the grace that is reaching more and more people may cause thanksgiving to overflow to the glory of God. Therefore we do not lose heart.

Though outwardly we are wasting away, yet inwardly we are being renewed day by day. For our light and momentary troubles are achieving for us an eternal glory that far out weighs them all. So we fix our eyes not on what is seen, but on what is unseen. For what is seen is temporary, but what is unseen is eternal.

Many years ago, I heard a teaching by Kay Arthur, Founder of Precepts for Life, in which she shared three very important things to remember when you find yourself in a season of suffering or persecution. I committed these to memory at that time and have found them to be extremely helpful in times of persecution. I encourage you to do the same.

1. **God promises that the suffering will never be more than you can bear.**

    1 Cor 10:12, *No temptation has seized you except what is common to man. And God is faithful; he will not let you be tempted beyond what you can bear. But when you are tempted, he will also provide a way out so that you can stand up under it.*

2. **The Lord Jesus Christ is with you and will never leave you or forsake you.**

    Hebrews 13:5 says, *Keep your lives free from the love of money and be content with what you have, because God has said, 'Never will I leave you; never will I forsake you.'*

3. **Know that your life cannot be taken, because it is held in God's hands.**

    Hebrews 2:14 says, *Since the children have flesh and blood, he too shared in their humanity so that by his death he might destroy him who holds the power of death that is, the devil.*

    Revelations 1:18 says, *I am the Living One; I was dead, and behold I am alive forever and ever! And I hold the keys of death and Hades.*

You can be content in the midst of challenging circumstances of any kind when your focus is on God and your relationship with Him. Without keeping your eyes on Jesus, however, you will not be able to respond in a manner that will transform suffering into the glory of God. Suffering will be suffering without glory. This is a key principle. It is only out of your intimate relationship with God that you will be able to respond this way. But then it is because of your relationship with Him that you are having the opportunity to respond. Your suffering is changed into glory as you respond:

1. **To God** rejoicing, counting it joy and giving thanks.

    1 Peter 4:12 tells us, *Dear friends, do not be surprised at the painful*

trial you are suffering, as though something strange were happening to you.

2. **To the person(s) causing the suffering,** in love without intimidation (1 Peter 3:14-15).

   In 1 Peter 2:20-25, we see Christ's example of how we are to **respond to suffering**—*But how is it to your credit if you receive a beating for doing wrong and endure it? But if you suffer for doing good and you endure it, this is commendable before God. To this you were called, because Christ suffered for you, leaving you an example that you should follow in his steps. He committed no sin, and no deceit was found in his mouth. When they hurled their insults at him, he did not retaliate; when he suffered, he made no threats. Instead, he entrusted himself to him who judges justly. He himself bore our sins in his body on the tree, so that we might die to sins and live for righteousness; by his wounds we have been healed. For you were like sheep going astray, but now you have returned to the Shepherd and Overseer of your souls.*

The bottom line is that anyone who walks with God will be persecuted at times. Jesus said, *If they persecuted Me, they will also persecute you* (John 15:20b). We should not be surprised. The enemy of our souls will work in any way he can, in any given situation, even using people in our congregations in order to persecute those he feels threatened by. If you have a desire to advance the Kingdom of God, to glorify God, to promote unity in the body of Christ and to grow in Christ's likeness, you will be persecuted. The powers of spiritual darkness will be at work, doing their best to thwart these plans. Satan would like to keep us distracted with persecution so that we do not fulfill God's purpose for our lives. But Satan is a created being and God is infinitely greater! The more we are persecuted, the stronger we become in Christ! The more attacks, the more grace God gives us and the more of His heavenly character we absorb.

Because of Christ we can be satisfied and experience an inward happiness, even in the midst of challenging circumstances. We can count it joy to share in the sufferings of Christ, because we know we will also share in His glory. As we respond out of love toward God by enduring, by not retaliating, by not making threats, and by entrusting ourselves to the One who judges fairly, we can know that the results will be eternal. God will be glorified. We will be purified. Others will be justified. All to the glory of God!

Experience Godliness God's Way

The Blessing: The Kingdom of Heaven; righteousness, peace and joy in the Holy Spirit (Romans 14:17)

The Recipient: Those who are persecuted because they belong to God and choose to do what is right before Him

So they went on their way from the presence of the Council, rejoicing that they had been considered worthy to suffer shame for His name.
–Acts 5:41 NASB

Reflect and Grow:

Resulting spiritual fruit: Self-control

Characterization of those persecuted for righteousness:
Committed to stand for Christ regardless what it may cost;
Entrust themselves and the circumstances of their life
to God knowing that as they share in Christ's sufferings,
they will also share in His glory

Opposite worldly attitude: Unfaithfulness

Opposing worldly value: Weak commitments

1. Consider the spiritual fruit produced when you cultivate this attitude. Think of a Scripture that you can sow as seed at times the opposite attitude tries to take root in your heart.

2. Notice the opposite worldly attitude. Compare this to Galatians 5:19-21. Are you being influenced by any of these ungodly vices?

3. Look at the characterization listed above for this beatitude and compare it to its opposing worldly value. How do they differ? Compare those who stand through persecution to the opposite world attitude. What area(s) or circumstance in your life exists that you need to make an intentional decision to lay down the worldly value and/or attitude to pick up the character trait of this beatitude?

4. To develop this attitude: Consider 2 Timothy 3:12; Mark 4:17; Matthew 10:24.

Things to Remember:

- Grow in your love for God and the hope of your calling in Christ Jesus.
- When your commitment to God provokes persecution, rejoice. You will share in Christ's glory.
- Don't take persecution personal. It is the Christ in you that is being persecuted.
- The persecution is a result of God's glory resting on you.
- Persecution within the church results from carnal and religious attitudes.
- When you are living with the truth reigning within your members, the darkness in people wants to hide.
- If you have a desire to advance the Kingdom of God, to glorify God, to promote unity in the body of Christ, to uphold the Word of God and/or to grow in Christ's likeness, you will be persecuted.
- The enemy uses people to persecute those he himself feels threatened by.

1. Read Jeremiah 38:6. Why is it that Jeremiah was persecuted?

2. Read Matthew 10:17-18 and John 9:28 and 9:34. What do these Scriptures tell us persecution may result from?

3. Read Mark 5:39-40. What form of persecution is found in this Scripture?

4. Read Acts 5:40-42. Are you willing to suffer for the gospel? What gives you the strength to do so? Consider Christians in other parts of the world, who suffer physical persecution for Christ even unto death, and pray for them. Don't forget to pray for their boldness and strength to stand.

5. Read Galatians 5:11. What did Paul's persecution prove?

6. Matthew 26:35 tells us that persecution does what ?

7. Read Acts 11:20-21. What do we see persecution resulted in?

8. What is the difference between suffering persecution for Christ and suffering because of wrongdoing? Is there a reward in the second situation?

9. Philippians 1:29 testifies, *For it has been granted to you on behalf of Christ not only to believe on him, but also to suffer for him.* How is it that we can consider suffering in our lives as a gift? Does considering suffering as a gift mean that we should do things to purposely attract suffering into our lives?

10. What are some ways other than jail or martyrdom we as Christians might suffer persecution in our everyday lives?

11. Why might someone living an intimate relationship with Christ suffer persecution in the form of insults, rejection, gossip etc. from both Christians and unbelievers?

12. How should we respond to persecution and insults?

13. Read Revelation 1:17-18. What does this Scripture reveal is available for us?

14. When will persecution end? Read Revelation 7:17.

Father, help me in the midst of persecution to overcome the world as You have overcome the world. Give me boldness and strength to stand and to proclaim the truth of the gospel even when there is risk of persecution. I lift those who are in the persecuted church now, and I ask that You raise a banner up over them. May their crisis and mine result in others coming to know You. In Jesus' name, Amen.

Others, like seed sown on good soil, hear the word, accept it, and produce a crop—thirty, sixty or even a hundred times what was sown.

–Mark 4:20

Chapter Fourteen

In Summary

Years ago, while in the sales profession, I attended a motivational sales conference, where Zig Ziglar spoke. Each day, he encouraged us to consider what we were thinking and what attitudes were forming within our minds concerning our lives, work and other situations we were faced with. He called this process a "check up from the neck up." Let me tell you, my friends, I have come to realize that if we are going to live a happy, blessed life, maturing in our walk with Christ, we need to have a regularly scheduled check-up concerning what is going on in our minds. We all need to keep a check on our attitudes. Remember, happiness, along with the blessed life, is hidden in godliness. Godliness is a devotion towards God seen in our attitudes which then manifest in our behavior. Godliness is God's greatest goal for us. He desires for us to conform to the image of Christ (Romans 8:29). Everything else flows out from this goal as we develop His attitudes, heart and mind.

One thing I like to do when I take a Sabbath day of rest is to ask God to show me any attitudes I had that week that were not in sync with Christ. As I begin to reflect back on the week's events, it never fails—God shows me areas where I need improvement. The wonderful thing is, I know that I don't have to try to change my attitudes all by myself. I only need to recognize and decide to change, realize my need for God, surrender to Him in the process and be intentional about training myself unto godliness. We train ourselves unto godliness through the spiritual disciplines of prayer, fasting, meditation, Bible study, worship and missions.

As we studied the Beatitudes, we looked at eight descriptions of attitudes we are to develop as followers of Christ. These beatitudes are in direct contradiction to the way the world lives; and as Jesus points out in the last beatitude, those who are making a serious effort to develop these traits will most likely experience various forms of opposition. However, if we are to grow in godliness and experience blessed happiness, our goal needs to be to become like Him. All those who are born again should have a desire to do so.

Godliness is a devotion towards God seen in our attitudes which then manifest in our behavior.

After conversion, the goal to conform our attitudes to God's begins with a decision and turning to God for help. We act in obedience, while asking God to change our hearts. Do not be discouraged as you find yourself faced with the same kind of situations you have dealt with in the past. Again, as Jesus did, when faced with temptation in the wilderness, sow Seed (the Word of God) needed for the situation. Remember, although it becomes easier with experience, we never reach a level where we never need to sow the Word for any given area of life. He will do a work in us illuminating, instructing, empowering us to choose the right behavior. And as we cooperate with Him, sowing seeds, He begins to bring forth a harvest of fruits of righteousness through our lives. Eventually we realize we have changed. The more we change, the more we realize we need to change more. It's not a feeling of condemnation or of anxiety; but a desire for oneness with Him.

We can relax in our journey with Him. He knows us, loves us and He told us that His yoke is easy. We realize He is a holy God, we are thankful for what He has done for us at the cross and we realize we need Him in our daily lives.

As we journey from glory to glory, we are able to rest as we abide in Christ, give our burdens to Him and take up His yoke. He has promised to be with us and never forsake us. He also promises that He will complete the work He has begun in us. Although we are diligent to train ourselves and exercise our spiritual muscles, there is no need for us to be anxious about our growth. He will perfect us. We need only to believe. It is up to us to believe and trust God to complete His good work in us because of our relationship with Christ through faith. Hebrews 4:10 says, *For the one who has entered*

His rest has himself also rested from his works, as God did from His. Herein we find rest. We do not trust in our works for our salvation. Salvation is found in Christ alone. Nor do we trust in works for our sanctification. We do not do good in an effort to earn favor with God. Nor do we do them to keep it. We do our works in response to our salvation and because we believe we are who God says we are. Therefore, there is no reason to be anxious. God has called us holy and is in the process of making us so. But our works are evidence of the confidence and hope we have in Christ.

The Israelites failed to believe that God would help them conquer the giants in the land. They looked at what they were able to do alone without God instead of what they were able to do with God. Thus they turned back from the promised land instead of moving forward and laying hold of it. We have seen that God has called us holy and expects us to live a godly life, therefore we can believe He will help us to conquer our giants. He has called us to perfection and will help us to be perfect. If we believe this, unlike the Israelites example, we will begin to walk according to the ways God has revealed to us. We will begin to take our thoughts captive and line our attitudes up with Christ's. We move forward as we make the decision to conform to His ways. James tells us that although our works do not save us, our works are evidence of our faith. Just as the Israelites, should have, could have moved into the promised land where they would have found God's power at work, we can move into God's promise of godliness. God will empower us and change us as we make the decision to do so.

Hebrews 4:11-12 says, *Therefore let us be diligent to enter that rest, so that no one will fall, through following the same example of disobedience. For the word of God is living and active and sharper than any two-edged sword, and piercing as far as the division of soul and spirit, of both joints and marrow, and able to judge the thoughts and intentions of the heart.* When in difficult and challenging situations or facing temptation, our own strength and efforts alone is never adequate; only Christ can see us through. His power saved us and it is His power that will keep us to the very end until He returns again.

However, because we love Christ and we are thankful for the gift of salvation, we should desire to make every effort by the grace of God to obtain everything Christ has made available to us this side of heaven. Every gift God offers involves the opportunity to choose and commit to His ways. God's Word demands of us to decide who we will live for. Our decision is seen in our actions. Some just listen to the Word and fail to apply it to their lives.

Let us be intentional to allow this living and powerful word coupled with the power of the Holy Spirit to shape us into the image of Christ. As we do, we will be all that God has called us to be while laying hold of all that God has made available to us in Christ.

A godly response to life's challenges becomes easier over time because when opportunities arise to challenge our attitudes, we have learned how to rely on God and what seeds to sow. We know that we just need to sow the right seed to ensure we reap the harvest of Christ-likeness in that particular situation.

This principle of sowing and reaping reminds me of when I started a workout routine. The first couple of weeks were murder. It took everything in me to force myself to do what I had committed to do. But as time went on, it became easier and easier until finally, it was even something I looked forward to. This is not to say there were not days that I wanted to relax in my routine and forget the exercise. Nor can we relax and fail to continue sowing seed. It is erroneous to think of our spiritual development as though we have passed a grade and will never struggle with our attitude or a temptation in any area ever again. Just as we are tempted to depart from physical training, we have temptations to depart from training ourselves in godliness as well. We are tempted when someone hurts us to sow un-forgiveness instead of seeds of mercy. We are tempted to hold onto our pride and personal independence instead of sowing humility. At times we are tempted to think our sin is not all that bad so we don't really need to repent of it. Sometimes we want to be served by others instead of serving others. We are tempted to demand our rights and display our power when God desires that we sow seeds of meekness and gentleness towards others so that we can harvest the fruit of peace.

Remember that God's ideal of perfection is not to reach a level where we no longer need to train or sow seed any longer. That is undoable. Just as Adam and Eve were created perfect, they remained perfect as long as they remained continually dependent on God. When they set out to walk in independence by taking the forbidden fruit, they lost their perfection. Therefore, in order to maintain a realization of our need for God, He allows multiple challenges to come our way to remind us that we need Him. As we go to Him and sow the seed He has provided for us, we produce multiple harvests of the same fruit, all over again. God's idea concerning godliness is that we continually sow the Word of God into our lives. His idea is that we choose to take our thoughts captive and change our attitudes to line up with those revealed to us in Christ. There will always be challenges to our attitudes, and, as there are, we have the opportunity to sow and produce another harvest of Christ-likeness. This means we are always dependent on God. Therefore, we do not need to feel like failures, because we are still being challenged with the same type of issues. It is all in God's plan of perfection, which is a plan that requires us to always need Him. So just relax, and continue sowing and reaping. You are doing fine. You are harvesting multiple crops of the same fruit. And, from the sowing to the harvest and every stage in between, God calls every stage of the spiritual fruit's growth "perfect."

For example, a number of years ago, I planted a garden of vegetables to include corn. I sowed my seed and in a few days a tiny green plant began to push through the ground. I had weeds to sprout as well in my garden, and I worked to remove them. My plants continued to grow until one day my corn was about 6' high but still no fruit. Then one day my crop was mature and producing corn. Although I was delighted at the harvest, every stage of growth prior to the harvest was necessary and perfect. This is how God sees us as we are devoted to Him. Perfect. We sow and reap, uprooting that which doesn't belong along the way. He sees each phase of growth as perfect as we remain committed to Him.

Young believers often find success and growth by accident, whereas, the more seasoned we are, the more we find that our growth comes by experience and deliberate action. If we want to mature in Christ, we must be diligent to sow Christ (the Word) and to be intentional about our goal. We sow these attitudes, as seen in the Sermon on the Mount, as we take our thoughts captive to the obedience of Christ (2 Cor 10:5). We are empowered by the Word and the Spirit of God as we have seen and read about in the book of Romans. Soon we begin to harvest Christ-likeness in our life. The Holy Spirit matures the seed we have sown and brings forth a harvest of love, joy, peace, patience, kindness, goodness, faithfulness, gentleness and self-control. We sow humility and love is produced again. We sow repentance and another harvest of joy springs forth. It is an amazing way to live. If we get the false idea that we have passed the grade for any of these attitudes, we will stop sowing. And when we do, we will begin to have crop failure. The harvest of Christ-likeness will stop and we find ourselves in a state of ungodliness.

We must continue to sow seeds of Christ's character, so that His likeness is harvested through our lives. When we sow God's spiritual seed of mercy (forgiveness) into our life we will reap the mature fruit of Christ's goodness. The weeds of un-forgiveness are uprooted and God is pleased that He sees

Christ's character. When we live out a life of faithfulness under persecution, we harvest the fruit of self-control. God looks at us and again says, "That's perfect." God's desire is a continual harvest of Christ-likeness, sowing and reaping over and over again. The false idea of perfection and one that is undoable is that we reach a level of perfection as though we have gone beyond a level to a higher level of being. If this were attainable, it would mean that we would no longer need God. This is not God's idea of perfection. We are to always be aware of our need for God (His Word and His Spirit) and our need to sow spiritual seed in order to reap the nature of Christ. This is God's idea of perfection. We can experience godliness in God's way, which is living life according to the garden pattern of sowing and reaping.

There is a corresponding fruit produced by the Holy Spirit for every Christ-like attitude we sow. As we continually sow these spiritual seeds to our every situation, the Holy Spirit will faithfully produce the character of Christ within us. We will see the evidence of this inward work in the outworking of the spiritual fruit of love, joy, peace, patience, kindness, goodness, faithfulness, gentleness and self-control. The development of the spiritual fruit is the work of the Holy Spirit. "Our transformation is His work." Yet, it is our responsibility to decide to change our attitudes and to sow the Word of God. We need to commit to a lifestyle of prayer, preparing the ground of our hearts for this supernatural growth to take place.

Understand that it is not our power and strength that changes us. We must rely on God's power. Just as we are saved by grace, at this point, the grace of God is the power of God that enables us to change. He sheds light on our attitudes revealing to us the areas of darkness within. Without this, we are deceived and blind to our ungodly attitudes. He then empowers us to cooperate with His work of transformation. We conform. He transforms. It is our decision to obey God due to our love for God that activates that power.

> **Galatians 5:6 AMP,** *For [if we are] in Christ Jesus, neither circumcision nor uncircumcision counts for anything, but only faith activated and energized and expressed and working through love.*

Do you see it? Faith activated, faith energized, faith expressed and faith working through love. As Christians, we should study love and learn what real love, God's kind of love looks like. We must ask God to pour His love into our hearts that we may love Him and love others as He does. Love is both a command and a fruit of the spirit. Therefore, we can begin practicing love even before we necessarily feel love until the fruit of God's love within us is perfected. Love will increase within us as our intimacy with and obedience to God increases.

We are able to walk in godliness because we have received the perfect sacrifice offered by Jesus' on the cross. When He died on the cross, He declared, "It is finished." His sacrifice was final, securing for us personal and intimate access to God forever. He is ever present to help us as we turn to Him. Jesus set us free from the power of sin and death enabling us to live out holiness in our daily lives on earth. God has set us apart for godly living that we may bring honor and glory to His name in all that we do. It is not accomplished in our power but by the power found in His immeasurable grace.

When we want to change, God helps us. We are enabled to change because Christ lives in us. He shows us what we are to conform to and then empowers us to do it. I hope you will make a decision today to activate that power by making a commitment to grow in Christ-likeness and begin to progress in God's priority goal for your life.

The Blessing: An intimate relationship with God where you experience His desires, thoughts and heart as your own; This is the blessed, happy and abundant life

The Recipient: The believer who allows the Word of God to challenge the way they live and intentionally sets a goal, with the help of the Holy Spirit, to become like Christ

Jesus prayed,
"Holy Father, protect them by the power of your name—the name you gave me—so that they may be one as we are one."
–John 17:11b

Reflect and Grow:

Things to Remember:

- As we conform, God transforms.
- We have multiple opportunities to sow the Word in order to have multiple harvests of Christ-likeness.

Seek and Apply:

1. Read Chapter 13 of 1 Corinthians. Ask the Holy Spirit to reveal to you how you are doing in your love walk. Without love, our faith for a Christ-like walk will lack. If it is lacking, humble yourself before the Lord. Seeds of humility produce the fruit of love in our lives.

2. Make a list and discuss a number of ways that love is evidenced in a person's life.

3. Why should we as Christians set a goal to grow in godliness?

4. Read Romans 12:2. Who is involved in transforming our minds?

5. Read Titus 3:5. – Whose work is being stressed in this verse regarding our transformation?

6. Read Galatians 5:22-23. How is this fruit produced in our lives?

7. What has been your ideal of living the Christian life in the past? Analyze the pros and cons of that ideal for spiritual formation. Think about and discuss the garden paradigm for living life. How does your previous way of living life differ from this one?

8. Does the garden principle make your burden feel lighter? What changes in your thinking and behavior are needed in order for you

Experience Godliness God's Way

to apply the garden principle of living and growing in godliness to your own life?

9. The Word of God invites us to action. Consider the invitation application of the following Scriptures to your life:

> Leviticus 4:2, 13, 22, 27 invites us to acknowledge our propensity to sin by nature and our need for God's forgiveness and grace to save and keep us.
>
> Leviticus 26:1-46 invites us to study and practice the Word of God.
>
> Leviticus 5:1; Luke 18:9-14 invites us to bring our sin into the open and deal with it according to the Word. Call it sin and repent of it. Do not justify it by comparing yourself with others. Only through acknowledging sin and seeking forgiveness can we be set free from its power.
>
> Leviticus 6:4,5 invites us to make restitution, when possible, for sins we have committed against others.
>
> Matthew 5:13-16; mark 9:50; Luke 11:33 invites us to recognize our responsibility for our actions, that they produce either a negative or positive effect; either do not or do glorify God.
>
> Matthew 22:15-22 invites us honor the Lord as the highest authority.
>
> 1 Timothy 2:4:7, 8, 12 invites us to discipline our whole selves and conduct ourselves in a godly manner.
>
> 1 Timothy 4:3-5 – The source of holiness is a personal relationship with Jesus and not a system of works. Therefore, reject teaching that bases holiness on works. That is holy that God has called holy and works are the outworking of that holiness.
>
> 2 Timothy 1:3 invites us to maintain a clear conscience
>
> 2 Timothy 2:15 invites us to commit to time studying The Word of God
>
> 2 Timothy 3:5 – Do not be deceived. Look for spiritual fruit in others.

Hebrews 4:1-10 invites us to receive and rest in the salvation Jesus' has provided by grace through faith and not works.

Hebrews 5:12-14 invites us to study the Word and determine to mature in your faith and walk.

Hebrews 10:32-39 invites us to endure suffering by holding onto God's promises. Remain faithful in your walk with God.

Hebrews 10:22 invites us to know that Jesus' sacrifice forever secured our personal and intimate access to God.

Prayer

Thank you, Father, that Your divine power has granted to us everything pertaining to life and godliness through the true knowledge of Christ who called us by His own glory and excellence. Thank You for Your precious and magnificent promises that by them we may become partakers of the divine nature, having escaped the corruption that is in the world by lust. (2 Peter 1:2-4) In Jesus' name, Amen.

A Final Thought

But we all, with unveiled face, beholding as in a mirror the glory of the Lord, are being transformed into the same image from glory to glory, just as from the Lord, the Spirit.

–2 Corinthians 3:18

As God is working out the life of godliness within you, for which He set you apart, remember He is pleased with you at every stage of your growth, as long as your life is devoted to Him. As you focus on Christ, and not your weaknesses, His strength will empower you to live a righteous life that will glorify Him. Just relax, stay committed no matter what happens and allow Christ's life to become yours.

Live for God's glory. Take time to enjoy Him. He is glorified through our enjoyment of Him. As you spend time with Him in this way, you surely will be transformed.

May the Lord cause you to increase and abound in love for Him and others; so that He may establish your heart without blame in holiness before our God and Father at the coming of our Lord Jesus with all His saints.

–1 Thessalonians 3:12-13

Love in Christ,

Sarah

Appendix A

A fun acrostic to help you stay on

The Path of Godliness

Remember...

G od is your source for a transformed life. He has set you apart for holiness.

O rder your steps according to God's Word and acceptance versus man's ideas and acceptance.

D ecide & determine to make God's priority goal for you, one of Christ-likeness, yours as well.

L ove God with all your heart, mind, soul and strength and love your neighbor as yourself.

I nclude in your life regularly, fellowship and the spiritual disciplines of prayer, bible study, meditation, fasting and missions.

N ever-cease to thank God for the free gift of eternal salvation; never-cease to worship Him; and never-cease to rely on His power, grace and strength for godly living.

E vangelize those God puts in your path, telling them the good news of Jesus Christ.

S tudy the Word of God, seek to know God's will and heart and your identity in Christ.

S tand in the good times and stand in times of suffering, remembering the promises of God will prevail.

Appendix B

How to Be Saved

The Bible says, ...*the gift of God is eternal life through Jesus Christ our Lord* (Romans 6:23). Heaven is a gift and like any gift, it is not earned and it is given even though not deserved. You could not do enough good deeds to earn a place in heaven. Ephesians 2:8, 9 says, *For by grace are you saved through faith; and not of yourselves: it is the gift of God: not of works, lest any man should boast.* You may ask why it is that no one can earn his way to heaven. The answer is, *All have sinned and come short of the glory of God* (Romans 3:23). Everyone has transgressed God's law with the sin or sin(s) of lying, lust, cheating, deceit, evil thoughts, immoral behavior and more. So man is unable to save himself. He cannot be good enough. Matthew 5:48 tells us, *Be ye therefore perfect, even as your Father which is in heaven is perfect.* Neither you nor I can meet this standard. However, in spite of our sin God in His mercy has loved us. ...*I have loved thee with an everlasting love....* (Jeremiah 31:3). God is love according to I John 4:8 and He does not want to punish us. But God is also just and therefore He must punish sin. He says, ... *(I) will by no means clear the guilty....* (Exodus 34:7) and ...*the soul that sinneth, it shall die* (Ezekiel 18:4). So God had this problem of loving us and not wanting to punish us; yet being a just and holy God He must punish sin. He solved this problem for us through Jesus Christ. The Bible tells us clearly that He is the infinite God-man. *In the beginning was the Word (Jesus)...and the Word (Jesus) was God. And the Word (Jesus) was made flesh, and dwelt among us....* (John 1:1, 14) So Jesus Christ came to earth and lived a perfect and sinless life. Then He died on the cross to pay the penalty of our sins and rose from the grave to purchase a place for us in heaven. *All we like sheep have gone astray; we have turned every one to his own way; and the LORD hath laid on Him (Jesus) the transgressions (sin) of us all* (Isaiah 53:6). Jesus Christ bore our sin in His body on the cross and now offers you eternal life (heaven) as a free gift.

To receive this free gift, you must have saving faith. Saving faith is not mere intellectual assent, like believing certain historical facts. The Bible says the devil believes there is one God, so believing there is one God is not saving faith. Saving faith is not mere temporal faith either. It is not trusting God in a temporary crisis situation such as financial, family or some physical need. These are things we can trust God for, but they are not saving faith!

Saving faith is trusting Jesus Christ alone for eternal life. It means resting upon Christ alone and what He has done rather than in what you or I have done to get us into heaven. ...*Believe (trust) on the Lord Jesus Christ and thou shalt be saved....* (Acts 16:31). This is the greatest story ever told about the greatest offer ever made by the greatest person who ever lived, Jesus Christ.

The question now is, would you like to receive Jesus Christ—the gift of eternal life? To do this you need to transfer your trust from what you have been doing to Christ on the cross and accept Christ as Savior by opening your heart and inviting Him in. He says, *Behold, I stand at the door, and knock: if any man hears My voice, and opens the door, I will come in to him....* (Revelation 3:20).

Receive Jesus Christ as Lord of your life by giving Him the driver's seat and control of your life—not the back seat.

Repent by turning from anything that is not pleasing to Him. He will reveal His will to you as you grow in your relationship with Him.

Now if this is what you really want you can go to God in prayer right where you are. You can receive His gift of eternal life through Jesus Christ right now. *For with the heart man believes unto righteousness; and with the mouth confession is made unto salvation. For whosoever shall call upon the name of the Lord shall be saved* (Romans 10:10, 13). If you want to receive the gift of eternal life through Jesus Christ, then call on Him, asking Him for this gift right now. Here's a suggested prayer: "Lord Jesus Christ, I know I am a sinner and do not deserve eternal life. But, I believe You died and rose

Appendix B

from the grave to purchase a place in heaven for me. Lord Jesus, come into my life; take control of my life; forgive my sins and save me. I repent of my sins and now place my trust in You for my salvation. I accept the free gift of eternal life."

If this prayer is the sincere desire of your heart, look at what Jesus promises to those who believe in Him: *Verily, verily, I say unto you, he that believeth on Me hath everlasting life* (John 6:47 KJV).

Welcome to God's family! *But as many as received Him, to them gave He power to become the sons of God, even to them that believe on His name* (John 1:12 NKJV).[25]

You now belong to God and if you have surrendered your life to Him, you are in the best hands you can be in—His hands! Now you can continue on in your search for satisfaction with an expectation to discover it!

Appendix C

Identity Scriptures for the Christian

Who You Really Are

Seek to know the real you…the one whom God has called you to be. God has identified who you really are. In His grace, begin to walk as this person.

I am accepted, secure and significant. I am…

II Corinthians 5:17 – A new Creation in Christ Jesus.

John 1:12 – God's child

John 15:15 – Christ's friend

Romans 5:1 – Justified

Colossians 1:14 – Redeemed and forgiven of all my sins

Ephesians 2:10 – God's workmanship created to do good works which He has prepared for me

Romans 8:17 – An heir of God in Christ Jesus

II Corinthians 5:21 – The righteousness of God in Christ Jesus. Reigning in life by Christ Jesus through the abundance of grace and the gift of righteousness…and I am a king and priest unto God

I Peter 2:9 – A royal priesthood, a holy nation, a person for God's own possession

1 Corinthians 6:17 – United with the Lord and one spirit with Him

1 Corinthians 6:19, 20 – Purchased with a price by God

1 Corinthians 12:27 – A member of Christ's body

Ephesians 1:5 – Adopted by God as a child of God

Ephesians 1:1 – A saint

Ephesians 2:18 – Able to access God directly through the Holy Spirit

Colossians 2:10 – Complete in Christ

Ephesians 2:10 – God's workmanship

Ephesians 3:12 – Confident and free to approach God at any time

Romans 8:1 & II Timothy 1:7 – Free from condemnation and the spirit of fear

II Timothy 1:7 – Filled with a spirit of power, love and sound, disciplined mind

Romans 8:37 & I John 5:4 – A conqueror and a world overcomer

Ephesians 1:3 – Blessed with every spiritual blessing

Philippians 4:19 – Free from want and lack, for God has liberally supplied my every need

John 15:5 – A branch of the vine and I bear much fruit

I Corinthians 3:16 & 6:19 – A temple of God and the Holy Spirit dwells in me

Romans 8:1, 2 – Free of condemnation

Romans 8:35 – assured of the love of God and nothing can separate me from it

Romans 8:28 – Assured God works all things in my life together for good

Philippians 3:20 – A citizen of heaven

I John 4:4 – Indwelt by the Greater One and I have overcome the evil one

Galatians 3:13 – Redeemed from the curse of the law

III John 2 – Prospering and in exceeding abundant health as my soul is prospering

Ephesians 4:24 – Created in righteousness and true holiness

I Corinthians 15:58 – Steadfast, unmovable, always abounding in the work of the Lord

Acts 13:52 – Continually filled with joy and the Holy Spirit

II Peter 2:24 & Is 53:5 – Healed by the stripes of Jesus and free from pain in my body

Romans 8:31 – Free from guilt charges against me

2 Corinthians 1:21, 22 – Established, anointed and sealed by God

Colossians 3:3 – Hidden with Christ in God

Appendix C

Philippians 3:20 – Being perfected by God

2 Timothy 1:7 – Free of fear, Sound in mind possessing a spirit of power and love

Hebrews 4:16 – A recipient of God's grace and mercy in my times of need

Ephesians 6:14 – Standing and acting on the truth of God's Word

Ephesians 4:29 – Speaking words of faith, which edify and minister grace to the hearer

II Corinthians 5:20 & Rom 8:14 – An Ambassador for Christ Jesus and I am led by the Holy Spirit

II Corinthians 5:7 – Walking by Faith and not by sight

II Peter 1:4 – A partaker of God's divine nature and have escaped the corruption of the world

II Corinthians 2:14 – Always triumphant in Christ Jesus

I Corinthians 15:57 – Always having and living in victory through my Lord Jesus Christ

John 15:16 – Chosen and appointed to bear fruit

2 Corinthians 5:17 – A minister of reconciliation for God

2 Corinthians 6:1, 1 Corinthians 3:9 – God's co-worker

Matthew 5:13-14 – The salt of the earth, the light of the world

Isaiah 54:14 – Far from oppression and fear; and terror shall not come near me

Psalm 1:3 – A tree of righteousness which yields much fruit and I am prospering

Philippians 4:6-7 – Free from anxiety and care

Ephesians 6:10 – Strong in the Lord and the power of His might

Ephesians 2:6 – Seated with Christ in the heavenly realm

Philippians 4:13 – Can do all things through Christ who strengthens me

Acts 1:8 – A personal witness of Christ

Endnotes

[1] W. E. Vine, *Expository Dictionary of New Testament Words* (Grand Rapids, MI: Zondervan Publishing House:1952), 162.

[2] Michael W.H. Holcomb, *Attainable Perfection*, Copyright© by Michael W.H. Holcomb. (Advantage Books 2009), All rights reserved, 23.

[3] Michael W.H. Holcomb, *Attainable Perfection*, Copyright© by Michael W.H. Holcomb. (Advantage Books 2009), All rights reserved, 24.

[4] Michael W.H. Holcomb, *Attainable Perfection*, Copyright© by Michael W.H. Holcomb. (Advantage Books 2009), All rights reserved, 28.

[5] Michael W.H. Holcomb, *Attainable Perfection*, Copyright© by Michael W.H. Holcomb. (Advantage Books 2009), All rights reserved, 30.

[6] The *American Heritage® Dictionary of the English Language*, Third Edition Copyright © 1996, 1992 by Houghton Mifflin Company. Published by Houghton Mifflin Company.

[7] Dr. Caroline Leaf, *Who Switched Off My Brain?* (Dallas, TX: 2008), Copyright© by Switch On Your Brain USA Inc. All rights reserved, Thanks to Dr. Caroline Leaf whose book deepened Scripture insights on taking thoughts captive.

[8] *New Spirit-Filled Life Bible*, Copyright© 1982 by Thomas Nelson, Inc. All rights reserved, 1410.

[9] Robert J. Morgan, *Nelson's Complete Book of Stories, Illustrations, & Quotes* (Nashville, TN: 2003), Copyright © by Robert J. Morgan. All rights reserved, 202.

[10] Robert J. Morgan, *Nelson's Complete Book of Stories, Illustrations, & Quotes* (Nashville, TN: 2003), Copyright © by Robert J. Morgan. All rights reserved, 456.

[11] humble. Dictionary.com. Dictionary.com Unabridged (v 1.0.1), Based on the *Random House Unabridged Dictionary*, © Random House, Inc. 2006. http://dictionary.reference.com/browse/humble (accessed: September 27, 2006).

[12] Clyde S. Kilby, *Minority of One: A Biography of Jonathan Blanchard* (Grand Rapids, MI: Eerdmans Publishing House, 1959), 38.

[13] Pastor Jonathan Goebel sermon illustration 2005, Manna Church, Lumberton, NC.

[14] Patrick Kavanaugh, *The Spiritual Lives of Great Composers* (Nashville: Sparrow Press, 1992), 13.

[15] Pastor Jonathan Goebel sermon illustration 2005, Manna Church, Lumberton, NC.

[16] A.W. Tozer, *The Pursuit of God* (Camphill, PA: Christian Publications, Inc. 1993), 104.

[17] A.W. Tozer, *The Pursuit of God* (Camphill, PA: Christian Publications, Inc. 1993), 104.

[18] *New Spirit-Filled Life Bible*, Copyright© 1982 by Thomas Nelson, Inc. All rights reserved, 1296.

[19] Pastor Dan Cormie at Sermon Central 2006, sermoncentral.com

[20] With thanks to Michael Fletcher for his many sermons emphasizing this truth.

[21] Cited by Luis Palau, *"Experiencing God's Forgiveness,"* Multnomah Press, 1984.

[22] Martin Luther, *Encyclopedia of Quotations* by R. Daniel Watkins (Peabody, Massachusetts: Hendrickson Publishers 2001), 654.

[23] J. I. Packer, *Knowing God* (Downers Grove IL: InterVarsity Press 1973), 23.

[24] Ken Sande, *The Peace Maker* (Grand Rapids, MI: Baker Books 2006), 263.

[25] The gospel rendering was taken from Booklet *EO83G* of *Evangelism Explosion Int'l.*

Now that you have read about God's idea of godliness, discover how to experience real satisfaction.

Together these two virtues will open to you a life of great gain!

Are you smiling on the outside but feel empty on the inside? Are you searching for something or someone to quench your desire for more?

Experience REAL Satisfaction will guide you off the merry-go-round of discontentment. This book reveals powerful biblical insights that when applied to your life, result in energy, peace and joy. Life becomes satisfying. Today is the day that can change the rest of your life.

Why remain dissatisfied when you can
Experience Real Satisfaction?

Available at Bookstores everywhere
and online at Amazon.com

Godliness with contentment is great gain.
– 1 Timothy 6:6

EICI – Empowered In Christ Institute
"Imparting Vision for transformation and devotion to Christ"

God's greatest goal for His children is Christ-likeness.
Since it is God's greatest goal for you, shouldn't it also be yours?

Taught LIVE Online - 8 session Units

If your heart's desire is to become like Christ,
this online training school is for you!

Personal Mentoring by phone,
IM and email is included!

Led by Pastors Jonathan and Sarah Goebel

Taught by anointed, faithful
and seasoned Christian Ministers

For More Information
Visit Our Website and Contact us
for the next scheduled session
www.eici@gmail.com

I would love to be the speaker at your next event

To Inquire
Email: sarahagoebel@gmail.com

Professional Life Coaching Services

As a certified professional life coach and biblical counselor, I am dedicated to help you navigate the storms and changes in your life as well as to help you successfully implement changes you desire for yourself.

Let me help you write the next chapter of your life story.

One-on-one and small group coaching sessions are available.

To Inquire:
Email: CoachSarah@gmail.com

I would love to hear from you!

Please take a minute or two to drop me a line on my blog
www.BlogwithSarah.com

and visit my website
www.SarahGoebel.com

Please let me know how God used this book in your life.

IF YOU SAID THE SALVATION PRAYER
while reading this book,
"Congratulations & Welcome to the Family!"
Let me know, and I will have a free gift for you.
ALSO
You can register for my FREE devotionals
and upcoming news at my website
www.SarahGoebel.com

If you are enjoying the messages I share, you may want to share my book(s) and website information with your friends.

I hope you will connect with me on Facebook.
Let me know you met me through reading
Experience Godliness God's Way.
Facebook: www.facebook.com/CoachSarah

If you feel led by the Lord to help support this ministry
you may do so online at
www.DeclaringHisAnswer.com
(My 501c3 covering) or to snail mail support,
visit this website for address information.

Your prayers for this ministry are welcomed and appreciated!

The On Assignment Publishing Vision

*Challenging Christian writers
to complete the assignment
God has put on their hearts*

Providing a vehicle for authors to proclaim
through fiction and non-fiction books the principles
of grace, truth and power found in Christ Jesus.

Challenging readers and authors to know God,
to grow in Christ-likeness and to
enjoy God as they grow in relationship with
Him and other Christians.

May Christ be glorified.

www.OnAssignmentPublishing.com

Sarah Ann Goebel

Sarah is happily married to Sr. Pastor Jonathan C. Goebel, is the mother of two adult children, and is a grandmother. She also enjoys having a puppy as a member of her family.

Her Qualifications:
Sarah is Board Certified as a Biblical Counselor through the International Board of Christian Counselors and a graduate of Grace College of Divinity. In addition to her Bible education, she has completed training for certification as a professional life coach and enjoys helping people navigate changes in their lives. She also graduated from Christian Leaders Authors & Speakers Services (CLASS) and enjoys sharing the Word of God at conferences and church services. In addition to *Experience Godliness God's Way*, Sarah authored *Experience Real Satisfaction*.

Her Ministry Passion:
As a minister of the Gospel and Christian conference speaker, Sarah's passion is SPIRITUAL FORMATION and equipping the saints to become fully devoted disciples of Christ. She desires to be a support to Pastors everywhere as she forthrightly, yet lovingly imparts passion for more of God and less of oneself through her one day seminar "Keys to Spiritual Formation." Attendees leave with an increased commitment for spiritual growth and walk of forgiveness and unity of spirit.

Sarah also is a great encourager imparting a knowledge of God's character and ways and bringing hope to the hopeless. She imparts to her listeners a greater trust in God's rule, acceptance of one's identity in Christ and empowerment to leave the past behind while pressing onward for the high call in Christ Jesus.

Sarah is potentially reaching people in countries all over the world through her online television and radio broadcasts. You can learn more about Sarah Goebel Ministries and Sarah's broadcasts at www.sarahgoebel.com

www.ingramcontent.com/pod-product-compliance
Lightning Source LLC
Chambersburg PA
CBHW032114090426
42743CB00007B/350